Illustrated Classics from India

**Over 86 million copies of over 400 titles sold worldwide!**

Amar Chitra Katha is a collection of illustrated classics that retell stories from Indian mythology, history, folktales and legends through the fascinating medium of comics. Over 430 stories from all over India have been told in this series that has been endorsed by educationists and recommended by teachers the world over.

Through a masterful blend of commentary, dialogue and illustration, Amar Chitra Katha presents complex historical facts and intricate mythology in a format that would appeal to children. They not only entertain, but also provide a fitting introduction to the cultural heritage of India. In a country so vast and varied, the series also serves as a medium for national integration, by introducing young readers to the rich cultural diversity of the country and highlighting the achievements of local heroes.

Amar Chitra Katha comics are like family heirlooms, passed down from generation to generation. These timeless illustrated classics are now also available online on www.amarchitrakatha.com. Start your own collection today!

No.1009 • Rs 195

## INDIA BOOK HOUSE PVT, LTD.

© India Book House Pvt.Ltd.1997, Reprinted: November 2007, ISBN 81-7508-194-5
Published and Printed by India Book House Pvt, Ltd, Mahalaxmi Chambers,
5th Floor, 22 Bhulabhai Desai Road, Mumbai 400 026, India.

Illustrated Classics From India

# The Churning of the Ocean

The story of how the devas discovered divine nectar and gained immortality is a popular legend that is dramatic as well as enthralling.

It was an ocean of milk that was churned by the devas and asuras to yield the celestial nectar, using the great mountain Mandara as the churning rod. The serpent Vasuki volunteered to be the cord. Lord Vishnu assumed the form of a tortoise and served as a pivot for Mandara to be whirled around on.

It took the benevolence of all the great deities to execute this complex task. Vishnu sent down cooling showers to abate the fiery smoke from Vasuki's mouth and Shiva consumed the fearful poison that arose from the waters. The legendary Airavata, Surabhi and Uchchhaishrava arose from the churning waters, as did many beautiful apsaras and goddesses.

This popular tale is found, with minor variations, in the Puranas as well as in the two epics. Our version of this great story is derived mainly from the Bhagawat Purana and the Mahabharata.

**Script: Toni Patel     Illustrations: Dilip Kadam     Cover: Dilip Kadam**

...DRA, THE ...HO RULES THE ...OACHING.

INDRA WAS SEATED ON THE CELESTIAL ELEPHANT AIRAVATA.

O INDRA! ACCEPT THIS GARLAND FROM WHICH, EVEN NOW, THE BEES ARE COLLECTING SWEET AMBROSIA!

...AND JOKINGLY PLACED IT ON THE BROW OF AIRAVATA.

AIRAVATA, INTOXICATED BY THE FRAGRANCE TOOK HOLD OF THE GARLAND WITH HIS TRUNK...

...LING IT TO THE GROUND.

SAGE DURVASA WAS FURIOUS.

O, INDRA, WHAT AN ACT OF FOLLY IS THIS! I PRESENTED YOU A GARLAND WHICH IS THE DWELLING PLACE OF SHREE, THE GODDESS OF FORTUNE. YET YOU HAVE SPURNED IT!

YOU IMAGINE THAT I AM JUST ANOTHER ASCETIC AND HAVE TREATED ME WITH DISRESPECT!

KNOW, THEREFORE, THAT JUST AS YOU HAVE CAST THE GARLAND TO THE GROUND SO ALSO SHALL YOUR POWER AS A RULER CRUMBLE TO THE GROUND!

INDRA WAS APPALLED AT WHAT HE HAD DONE.

DISMOUNTING FROM HIS ELEPHANT HE BOWED HUMBLY BEFORE DURVASA.

SINLESS DURVASA, THIS ACT WAS DONE IN A MOMENT OF WEAKNESS. PLEASE FORGIVE ME!

BUT DURVASA WAS UNYIELDING.

I AM NOT COMPASSIONATE OF HEART, NOR DO I FORGIVE EASILY. I WILL NOT RELENT. YOU WHO ARE SO ARROGANT BY NATURE—DO YOU EXPECT ME TO ACCEPT YOUR NEW-FOUND HUMILITY?

FROM THAT DAY ONWARDS, PLANTS AND HERBS BEGAN TO WITHER. INDRA AND THE GODS LOST THEIR VIGOUR.

I FEEL DRAINED OF ALL ENERGY!

THERE IS NO ZEST IN LIFE ANY MORE!

OH, HOW COULD DURVASA HAVE BEEN SO HARSH!

IN THIS SITUATION, IT WAS THE ASURAS, THE ENEMIES OF THE DEVAS, WHO BENEFITED. THEY TAUNTED THE DEVAS.

YOU PROUD AND ARROGANT DEVAS! COME, FIGHT WITH US!

SO YOU HESITATE! WEAKLINGS!

THE DEVAS WERE FORCED TO ACCEPT THE CHALLENGE, THOUGH THEY WERE UNWILLING.

TAKE THAT!

AND THAT!

GREAT NUMBERS OF DEVAS WERE FELLED AND COULD NOT RISE AGAIN. THE REST, HEADED BY AGNI, THE GOD OF FIRE, FLED.

THEY DID NOT STOP TILL THEY CAME TO THE REGIONS OF BRAHMA.

OH, HOW WEAK AND TIRED I FEEL!

BRAHMA'S COURT WAS ON THE CREST OF THE SHINING MOUNT MERU. IT WAS FULL OF GRACEFUL TREES, FRAGRANT FLOWERS AND COOL STREAMS. BUT THE DEVAS WERE NOT SOOTHED EVEN BY THE SOFT BREEZE.

NOTHING INTERESTS ME ANY MORE, NOT EVEN THE MELODIOUS SINGING OF THE BIRDS!

THEY NOW APPROACHED BRAHMA.

O BRAHMA, LORD OF ALL CREATIONS, PLEASE SAVE US! TELL US WHAT TO DO AND WE WILL CERTAINLY DO IT. ONLY FREE US FROM SAGE DURVASA'S CURSE.

BRAHMA WAS MOVED BY THEIR SAD PLIGHT. HE MEDITATED FOR A WHILE...

...AND REMEMBERED THE OMNIPOTENT VISHNU.

THEN—

LET US SEEK THE HELP OF THE ONE, TO WHOM ALL THE GODS, THE ASURAS, THE ANIMALS, THE BIRDS, TREES AND EVEN I MYSELF... OWE OUR EXISTENCE. LET US SEEK VISHNU'S HELP.

COME, I WILL TAKE YOU TO HIM MYSELF.

WHEN BRAHMA HIMSELF LEADS US, HOW CAN WE FAIL!

WHEN THEY ARRIVED IN VAIKUNTHA, THE ABODE OF VISHNU, SO DAZZLED WERE THEY BY HIS BRILLIANCE, THAT THEY COULD NOT SEE THE FORM OF THE LORD.

WE BOW TO YOU...

WE BOW TO YOU UNCHANGING ONE...!

THE DEVAS WORSHIPPED VISHNU.

O THOU FOREMOST OF THE PURUSHAS!

OH, THOU ALL-KNOWING ONE!

FINALLY THEY WERE ABLE TO SEE HIM. HE WAS AS LUSTROUS AS A THOUSAND SUNS.

O, ALL-KNOWING BEING, SINCE NOTHING REMAINS HIDDEN FROM YOU, NEITHER PAST NOR PRESENT, YOU KNOW OF OUR PLIGHT.

HELP US THEREFORE AND GIVE US VICTORY AGAINST THE ASURAS.

LORD VISHNU WAS SILENT FOR A WHILE, THEN—

LISTEN TO ME CAREFULLY AND ALL WILL BE WELL WITH YOU.

YOUR ENEMIES HAVE OBTAINED VICTORY OVER YOU. SO, FOR THE MOMENT, YOU MUST MAKE PEACE WITH THEM.

HOW CAN WE DO THAT? THEY TAKE UNFAIR ADVANTAGE OF US AT EVERY TURN.

IT IS BETTER TO MAKE PEACE WITH ENEMIES, EVEN AS A SERPENT WILL MAKE FRIENDS WITH A MOUSE, IF NECESSARY.

BUT, LORD, WE ARE AFRAID TO GO NEAR THEM!

THAT IS WHY I SAY YOU MUST FIRST MAKE PEACE WITH THEM. THEN YOU MUST ENDEAVOUR TO CHURN UP THE NECTAR OF IMMORTALITY FROM THE OCEAN.

GET THOSE VERY ASURAS TO HELP YOU TO OBTAIN IT. ONCE YOU HAVE PARTAKEN OF IT, YOU WILL HAVE NOTHING TO FEAR FROM THEM EVER AGAIN!

BUT THEN, IF THE ASURAS HELP US WITH THE CHURNING, WON'T THEY ALSO HAVE THE ADVANTAGE OF THE NECTAR?

NO! THOUGH THEY WILL HELP WITH THE CHURNING, THE NECTAR WILL NOT BE THEIRS!

THE DEVAS WERE PLEASED WITH VISHNU'S ADVICE. THEY BOWED IN REVERENCE TO HIM.

WE WILL INVITE THE ASURAS TO JOIN US IN CHURNING THE OCEAN.

THE DEVAS WENT TO BALI, THE KING OF THE ASURAS. HE WAS RESTING AFTER HAVING CONQUERED THE THREE WORLDS.

LOOK AT THOSE WEAKLINGS, BEREFT OF ARMOUR AND WEAPONS!

LET'S STRIKE THEM DOWN!

NO! DO NOT DRAW YOUR WEAPONS. IT IS TIME TO MAKE PEACE WITH OUR ENEMIES.

BESIDES THEY OBVIOUSLY HAVE SOMETHING TO SAY TO US. SOME SCHEME FOR OUR MUTUAL BENEFIT PERHAPS?

SPEAK! WHY HAVE YOU COME HERE, AT GREAT RISK TO YOURSELVES? HAVE YOU SOME PROPOSALS TO MAKE?

WE HAVE, O WISE AND ILLUSTRIOUS KING!

WELL, GO ON THEN.

FIRST TELL US— ARE YOU INTERESTED IN OBTAINING THE CELESTIAL NECTAR, THE DRINK THAT IMPARTS IMMORTALITY?

THE CELESTIAL NECTAR!

HE'S ASKING US IF WE WOULD LIKE TO HAVE THE NECTAR!

OF COURSE, WE HAVE ALWAYS BEEN INTERESTED BUT EVERYONE KNOWS IT IS ALMOST IMPOSSIBLE TO OBTAIN IT.

WELL, WE HAVE DISCOVERED THE WAY TO DO IT. FIRST OF COURSE WE HAVE TO CHURN THE OCEAN OF MILK...

HERE IS OUR PLAN. WILL YOU HELP US?

HMMM....A GOOD PLAN. VERY INTERESTING!

BALI DISCUSSED THE PLAN WITH OTHER ASURA LEADERS, SHAMBARA, ARISHTANEMI, PAULOMA AND KALAKEYA.

DON'T YOU THINK THE PLAN IS A GOOD ONE?

YES, IT IS.

SO, FOR THE MOMENT, THE DEVAS AND THE ASURAS MADE A CONTRACT OF FRIENDSHIP.

LET US START MAKING OUR PREPARATIONS.

THEY WENT TOGETHER TO THE OCEAN OF MILK...

...AND THEY CAST ALL SORTS OF MEDICINAL HERBS INTO IT.

WE ARE READY, BUT THE OCEAN IS LIKE A MIGHTY CHURNING POT. WHAT SHALL WE CHURN IT WITH?

ONLY A MOUNTAIN WOULD DO AS A CHURNING ROD!

LORD VISHNU TOLD US TO UPROOT MOUNT MANDARA FOR THIS PURPOSE.

THAT'S RIGHT.

LET'S TRY AND UPROOT MOUNT MANDARA AND USE IT AS A CHURNING ROD.

THE MAJESTIC MOUNT MANDARA ADORNED WITH CLOUD-TOPPED PEAKS EXTENDED ELEVEN THOUSAND YOJANAS ABOVE THE GROUND AND WAS AS DEEPLY EMBEDDED IN THE EARTH.

INDRA AND THE DEVAS ALONG WITH BALI AND THE ASURAS UPROOTED MOUNT MANDARA...

...AND BEGAN TO CARRY IT TOWARDS THE OCEAN. ALTHOUGH THEY WERE VERY STRONG, THEY PANTED AND GASPED UNDER ITS WEIGHT.

IT'S SO HEAVY!

OH! WHY DID WE EVER EMBARK ON THIS PROJECT?

ON AND ON THEY WENT, OVER A GREAT DISTANCE.

OH! I AM EXHAUSTED! I CANNOT GO ANY FARTHER.

NOR... I!

OR I!

IN THE END, UNABLE TO HOLD OUT ANY LONGER, THEY DROPPED THE MOUNTAIN AND A LARGE NUMBER OF DEVAS AND ASURAS WERE CRUSHED UNDER IT.

THE CRIES OF THE ASURAS AND DEVAS INTERMINGLED.

HELP!

HELP!

WHAT SHALL WE DO NOW?

WE ARE NOWHERE NEAR COMPLETION OF OUR TASK!

BOTH THE ASURAS AND THE DEVAS WERE IN DESPAIR.

SO MANY OF OUR FRIENDS HAVE BEEN CRUSHED AND INJURED!

BUT LORD VISHNU, WHO SAW ALL THIS, ARRIVED ON HIS VEHICLE, GARUDA.

IT'S LORD VISHNU!

LORD VISHNU!

HIS HEALING GLANCE FELL ON THEM, AND THE INJURED DEVAS AND ASURAS WERE REVIVED.

OH, PAULOMA! YOU ARE WELL AGAIN!

OH, AGNI! HOW GLAD I AM TO SEE YOU ABLE TO STAND UP AGAIN!

THEN LORD VISHNU EFFORTLESSLY RAISED THE MOUNTAIN WITH ONE HAND...

...AND PLACED IT ON THE BACK OF GARUDA.

VISHNU HIMSELF THEN MOUNTED GARUDA AND PROCEEDED TOWARDS THE OCEAN OF MILK.

ON REACHING THERE, GARUDA GENTLY PLACED THE MOUNTAIN IN THE OCEAN...

...AND THEN FLEW AWAY. LORD VISHNU REMAINED BEHIND.

THEN THE DEVAS AND ASURAS WENT TO VASUKI, THE KING OF THE SNAKES.

O, VASUKI, COME HELP US TO CHURN THE MIGHTY OCEAN AND YOU SHALL ALSO PARTAKE OF THE NECTAR.

CERTAINLY! I WILL COME AND ACT AS A CHURNING ROPE.

SO VASUKI WENT WITH THEM AND ALLOWED THEM TO BIND HIM ROUND MOUNT MANDARA.

GOOD! WE'RE NOW READY!

THEN LET'S BEGIN THE CHURNING!

INDRA AND THE DEVAS THEN PROCEEDED TOWARDS THE HEAD OF VASUKI.

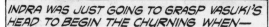

INDRA WAS JUST GOING TO GRASP VASUKI'S HEAD TO BEGIN THE CHURNING WHEN—

STOP! WHY SHOULD YOU HOLD THE HEAD?

WE WILL HOLD THE HEAD!

INDRA HID A SMILE AND QUIETLY WENT WITH THE DEVAS TO HOLD VASUKI'S TAIL INSTEAD.

JUST AS YOU LIKE, FRIENDS. WE SHALL NOT QUARREL ON SUCH A SMALL ISSUE!

WHEN BOTH THE GROUPS HAD TAKEN THEIR PLACES, THE ASURAS AT THE HEAD AND THE DEVAS AT THE TAIL OF VASUKI...

...THE CHURNING BEGAN.

WHIRR--WHIRR!

BUT ALAS! THERE WAS NO SUPPORT UNDER MOUNT MANDARA AND BECAUSE OF ITS IMMENSE WEIGHT, IT GRADUALLY SLIPPED DOWN TO THE BOTTOM OF THE OCEAN.

THE MOUNTAIN WON'T TURN!

THE MOUNTAIN IS SLIPPING FROM OUR GRASP!

NO! IT IS SLIPPING DOWN DEEPER AND DEEPER.

HELP! HELP!

ONCE AGAIN VISHNU CAME TO THEIR AID. ASSUMING THE FORM OF A GIGANTIC TORTOISE, ALMOST LIKE A HUGE ISLAND, VISHNU DIVED TO THE BOTTOM OF THE OCEAN...

...AND HELD MOUNT MANDARA UP ON HIS BACK.

BEGIN THE CHURNING!

THROUGH THE GRACE OF LORD VISHNU, THE DEVAS AND THE ASURAS AND VASUKI FELT A RENEWED STRENGTH WITHIN THEM AND THEY CHURNED FASTER AND FASTER.

THEN FIRE AND SMOKE ISSUED FROM THE THOUSAND MOUTHS OF VASUKI.

THESE FIERY PUFFS OF SMOKE ENGULFED THE ASURAS WHO WERE NEAR THE HOODS OF THE SNAKE.

I CAN'T BREATHE!

THESE FUMES ARE SUFFOCATING US!

LOOK! ALL OUR GREAT LEADERS PAULOMA, KALEYA, ILVALA SO PALE AND FAINT! THEY LOOK LIKE SHRIVELLED SHRUBS BURNT DOWN BY A FOREST FIRE!

THE DEVAS TOO WERE AFFECTED BY THE FUMES, BUT VISHNU SENT DOWN COOLING SHOWERS TO REVIVE THEM.

STILL THE DEVAS AND ASURAS CONTINUED THEIR TASK AND AS THEY CHURNED, A WHOLE HOST OF FISHES, SNAKES, WHALES WERE CHURNED UP TOO.

THEN THERE AROSE A FEARFUL POISON. IT SPREAD LIKE A THICK PALL OVER THE EARTH.

THIS IS THE TERRIBLE POISON, HALAHALA!

IT WILL SOON COVER THE WORLD AND KILL ALL ITS CREATURES!

THIS TIME THEY SENT UP A CRY TO LORD SHIVA—

LORD SHIVA WE ARE DYING! PLEASE HELP US!

INSTANTLY SHIVA HEEDED THEIR CALL. GATHERING UP ALL THE POISON IN THE PALM OF HIS HAND...

...HE SWALLOWED IT AND HELD IT IN HIS THROAT.

THE POISON MADE HIS THROAT BLUE AND BECAME AN ORNAMENT OF SHIVA. FROM THAT TIME ON HE HAS BEEN KNOWN AS NILAKANTHA.

WE SALUTE YOU, O NILAKANTHA, FOR RESPONDING TO OUR PRAYER!

THE DEVAS AND ASURAS RESUMED THEIR CHURNING. BEFORE LONG THERE AROSE FROM THE OCEAN SURABHI, THE DIVINE COW, UCHCHHAISHRAVA, THE HORSE WHITE AS THE MOON AND AIRAVATA, THE WHITE ELEPHANT WITH FOUR TUSKS. THEY WERE FOLLOWED BY A BEVY OF BEAUTIFUL APSARAS. LATER EMERGED THE CELESTIAL PARIJATA TREE AND VARUNI THE GODDESS OF WINE, ROLLING HER INTOXICATING EYES.

THEN **SHREE** AROSE FROM THE OCEAN, GRACEFUL AND EFFULGENT.

HER BEAUTY WAS SUCH AS TO STIR THE MINDS OF THE DEVAS AND ASURAS. ALL OF THEM WERE ANXIOUS TO BE OF SERVICE TO HER.

GANGA AND OTHER HOLY RIVERS BROUGHT WATER IN GOLDEN JARS FOR HER ABLUTIONS.

VASANTA, THE GOD OF SPRING, BROUGHT FRUITS AND FLOWERS.

THE APSARAS BEGAN TO DANCE FOR HER.

THE CLOUDS RAINED MUSIC FROM A VARIETY OF INSTRUMENTS.

VARUNA, LORD OF THE WATERS, BROUGHT HER THE CELEBRATED VAIJAYANTI GARLAND.

WHEN THE AUSPICIOUS CEREMONIES WERE COMPLETED, SHREE MOVED HERE AND THERE LOOKING FOR THE ONE WHO IS THE REPOSITORY OF ALL GOOD QUALITIES.

IN THE END, SHE CHOSE LORD VISHNU, WHO IS PERFECT IN EVERY WAY.

SHE PLACED THE BEAUTIFUL VAIJAYANTI GARLAND ROUND HIS NECK.

VISHNU, LORD OF THE THREE WORLDS, ACCEPTED HER.

THE CHURNING CONTINUED.

WHIRR--WHIRR!

FINALLY DHANVANTARI, THE DIVINE PHYSICIAN, CAME FORTH, HOLDING THE VESSEL OF CELESTIAL NECTAR.

AT LAST! THE DIVINE ELIXIR!

THE ASURAS GAVE A GREAT ROAR...

...AND TOOK THE PRECIOUS VESSEL FROM HIM BY FORCE.

ALL IS LOST. O, LORD VISHNU, SAVE THE PRECIOUS NECTAR!

VISHNU AT ONCE ASSUMED THE BEWITCHING FORM OF MOHINI, THE ENCHANTRESS.

MEANWHILE, THE ASURAS HAD BEGUN QUARRELLING AMONG THEMSELVES OVER THE JAR OF NECTAR.

SUDDENLY, THEY SAW MOHINI APPROACHING THEM WITH SWEET LOOKS AND ENCHANTING SMILES.

INTOXICATED WITH HER BEAUTY, THE ASURAS BEGAN TO FOLLOW HER.

SUCH GRACE!

SHE'S BEAUTIFUL!

WHY DON'T WE ASK HER TO DISTRIBUTE THE NECTAR TO US?

23

...SO PLEASE TAKE THIS DRINK AND DISTRIBUTE IT EQUALLY BETWEEN US!

ALL RIGHT, BUT YOU MUST PROMISE TO ABIDE BY MY DECISION, EVEN IF YOU DON'T LIKE IT.

NOTHING YOU DO WILL DISPLEASE US!

GIVING THEM THIS DRINK WOULD BE LIKE GIVING MILK TO POISONOUS SNAKES. NO, NO, THEY SHALL NOT HAVE IT!

MEANWHILE THE DEVAS AND ASURAS HAD ARRANGED THEMSELVES INTO TWO ROWS, QUIETLY WAITING FOR HER TO BEGIN.

MOHINI FIRST GAVE THE NECTAR TO ALL THE DEVAS TO DRINK...

...WHILE SMILING BEWITCHINGLY AT THE ASURAS. AND THE ASURAS WERE CONTENT WITH THE SMILES SHE FLASHED AT THEM.

BUT ONE OF THE ASURAS WHOSE NAME WAS RAHU, BECAME SUSPICIOUS.

SHE HAS NO INTENTION OF GIVING US THE NECTAR!

SO RAHU ASSUMED THE FORM OF DEVA AND QUIETLY CROSSED OVER.

FORTUNATELY, SURYA, THE SUN, AND SOMA, THE MOON, WERE WATCHFUL.

WAIT! HE'S NOT A DEVA!

NO, NO, I KNOW HIM! HE IS THE ASURA, RAHU!

THE NECTAR HAD BARELY REACHED RAHU'S THROAT. INSTANTLY VISHNU HURLED HIS CHAKRA AT HIM TO CUT OFF THE WELL-ADORNED HEAD OF THE ASURA.

AS THE HUGE HEADLESS TRUNK OF THE ASURA FELL DOWN, IT CAUSED THE EARTH TO QUAKE AND THE MOUNTAINS TO RUMBLE.

AND THE SEVERED HEAD OF THE ASURA ROSE TO THE SKY ROARING HORRIBLY.

TO THIS DAY THERE IS A DEADLY FEUD BETWEEN THE HEAD OF RAHU AND THE SUN AND THE MOON AND HE SWALLOWS THEM UP AT REGULAR INTERVALS, CAUSING ECLIPSES.

AT LAST, THE TRUTH DAWNED ON THE ASURAS!

THAT'S NO ENCHANTRESS! THAT'S VISHNU!

WE'VE BEEN TRICKED!

THEY BEGAN TO SCREAM AND MAKE A TERRIFIC DIN.

GIVE US THE NECTAR!

IT'S OURS!

AMID GREAT TUMULT AND EXCITEMENT MANY MORE OF THE GODS QUICKLY PARTOOK OF THE NECTAR WHICH THEY SO GREATLY DESIRED AND THEY BECAME IMMORTAL.

MEANWHILE THE ASURAS HAD BEEN ARMING THEMSELVES WITH VARIOUS WEAPONS.

THEN, ON THE SHORES OF THE OCEAN, BEGAN THE GREAT BATTLE BETWEEN THE DEVAS AND THE ASURAS.

SHARP POINTED JAVELINS AND LANCES WERE HURLED AT THE ASURAS.

THE ASURAS DIED IN LARGE NUMBERS THEIR HEADS ADORNED WITH BRIGHT GOLD FELL ON THE FIELD OF BATTLE.

WAR CRIES AND CRIES OF PAIN INTERMINGLED.

ATTACK!

PIERCE!

CUT!

KILL! KILL!

AT THE HEIGHT OF THIS FIERCE BATTLE, VISHNU ENTERED THE FIELD.

THEY SEEM EVENLY MATCHED. THE DEVAS NEED MY HELP.

AS SOON AS HE THOUGHT OF IT, HIS OWN INCOMPARABLE DISCUS, THE SHINING SUDARSHANA CHAKRA, CAME THROUGH THE SKY.

VISHNU AIMED THE SUDHARSHANA AT THE ASURAS. IT FLEW EVERYWHERE DESTROYING THOUSANDS OF ASURAS.

AT OTHER TIMES, IT BLAZED LIKE FIRE AND BURNED EVERYTHING AROUND IT.

BUT THE ASURAS WERE NOT YET DAUNTED. THEY ROSE SKYWARDS...

...AND HURLED HUGE MOUNTAINS AT THE DEVAS.

THE MOUNTAINS COLLIDING WITH EACH OTHER PRODUCED A TREMENDOUS UPROAR.

THE EARTH AND THE FORESTS BEGAN TO TREMBLE.

AGAIN THE DIVINE VISHNU CAME TO THE AID OF THE DEVAS. SHOOTING GOLDEN-HEADED ARROWS AT THE FALLING MOUNTAINS, HE REDUCED THEM TO DUST.

THE ASURAS WERE DEFEATED. THEY COULD FIGHT BACK NO MORE. SHRIEKING LOUDLY, SOME OF THEM ENTERED THE BOWELS OF THE EARTH, WHILE...

...OTHERS PLUNGED INTO THE OCEAN.

THE VICTORIOUS DEVAS PUT MOUNT MANDARA BACK IN ITS OLD PLACE AND DID OBEISANCE TO IT.

THEN THE SKIES RESOUNDED WITH JOYOUS SHOUTS AS THE DEVAS, HAVING BEEN RENDERED PERFECT AFTER DRINKING THE CELESTIAL NECTAR, RETURNED TO THEIR OWN ABODES.

**THE MAKING OF AMAR CHITRA KATHA**

**Script:**
Margie Sastry

**Illustrations:**
C. D. Rane

THE IDEA OF CREATING THE AMAR CHITRA KATHA COMICS ORIGINATED IN THE MIND OF THE EDITOR, ANANT PAI.

OVER 436 TITLES HAVE BEEN PUBLISHED SO FAR.

ALL NEW IDEAS ARE DISCUSSED WITH THE AMAR CHITRA KATHA EDITORIAL TEAM.

I THINK OUR NEXT TITLES SHOULD BE RAMAYAN. WHICH SOURCE SHOULD WE USE? VALMIKI OR TULSIDAS?

THE DISCUSSION RAISES MANY QUERIES …

…THAT CALL FOR SERIOUS RESEARCH FROM PRIMARY SOURCES.

MYTHOLOGY

HISTORY

THIS PROCESS IS FOLLOWED FOR ALL TITLES. FROM HISTORY AND MYTHOLOGY, TO LEGEND AND BIOGRAPHY.

WHEN THE SOURCE OF THE STORY IS DECIDED, A SCRIPTWRITER IS ASSIGNED THE TASK.

THIS IS THE SOURCE AND THESE ARE THE EDITORIAL GUIDELINES.

WOW! THE PROCESS IS MORE METICULOUS THAN I IMAGINED!

A STRINGENT EDITORIAL POLICY IS ESSENTIAL TO ESTABLISH QUALITY CONTROL.

THE SYNOPSIS OF EACH TITLE MUST BE APPROVED BEFORE THE COMIC IS CREATED, COMPLETE WITH COMMENTARY PANELS AND DIALOGUES.

BIRBAL'S COMMENTS MUST BE WITTY, AKBAR'S WRY YET REGAL.

THE DIALOGUES AND THOUGHTS OF EACH CHARACTER REFLECT THEIR PERSONALITY, AGE AND STATUS.

THE STORY IS SCRIPTED IN 30-32 PAGES, EACH WITH 5-6 PANELS. THE DIALOGUES SHOULD REFLECT THE ERA IN WHICH THE STORY IS SET AND ALSO CARRY THE STORY FORWARD.

NOW THE SCRIPT-WRITER MUST ADD DETAILED VISUAL NOTES FOR THE ARTIST FOR EACH PANEL.

THE ARTIST RECEIVES THE SCRIPT WITH SEVERAL BOOKS AND PICTURES FOR REFERENCE IN ORDER TO CREATE AUTHENTIC ARTWORKS.

WITH DRAMATIC DETAIL AND VIVID IMAGINATION, THE ARTIST BRINGS THE CHARACTERS TO LIFE ON PAPER.

THE PENCILLED ARTWORKS ARE THOROUGHLY SCRUTINISED FOR CONTINUITY AND AUTHENTICITY. THE ARCHITECTURE, DRAPERY AND COSTUMES MUST CORRESPOND TO THE PERIOD IN WHICH THE STORY IS BASED. THE ILLUSTRATIONS ALSO EXPRESS EMOTIONS.

MEANWHILE, THE SCRIPT IS SENT TO LANGUAGE EXPERTS AND SOMETIMES TO SUBJECT EXPERTS TOO.

CORRECTIONS ARE CARRIED OUT IN THE ARTWORKS AND THE SCRIPT WHEREVER NECESSARY.

THE LETTERING ARTISTS PUT WORDS IN THE MOUTHS AND THOUGHTS IN THE HEADS OF THE CHARACTERS.

THE PAGES COME ALIVE AS THE COLOURING ARTISTS ADD VIBRANT SHADES TO THE ARTWORKS.

THE COMPLETED ARTWORKS ARE CHECKED BY THE EDITORIAL TEAM AND MUST FINALLY PASS THE CRUCIAL TEST OF THE EDITOR'S TABLE.

ONCE THE APPROVAL OF THE EDITOR IS OBTAINED, THE COMIC IS READY TO GO TO THE PRINTER SO THAT THOUSANDS OF COLOURFUL COMICS CAN REACH OUR AVID READERS !

# Classic Collections

The immortal tales of Amar Chitra Katha
are now available as 3-in-1 digests with a special
selection of three delightful tales in one comic book.

| | |
|---|---|
| Tales from the Panchatantra | Matchless Wits |
| Tales of Birbal | More Tales from the Jatakas |
| More Tales of Birbal | Vishnu to the Rescue |
| Great Plays of Kalidasa | Buddhist Tales |
| Great Sanskrit Plays | More Buddhist Tales |
| Great Indian Emperors | Tales told by Sri Ramakrishna |
| Vishnu the Saviour | Further Tales from the Jatakas |
| Ranas of Mewar | The Sons of the Pandavas |

**Each 96-page digest is now available at a special online price of
Rs 68 (MRP Rs 80) at www.AmarChitraKatha.com. Start your collection today!**

## INDIA BOOK HOUSE

Mahalaxmi Chambers, 5th Floor, 22 Bhulabhai Desai Road, Mumbai 400 026, India.
Tel.: 2352 3409, 2352 5636  Fax: 2353 8406  E-mail: info@amarchitrakath.com

# Tales of Vishnu

Illustrated Classics From India

# Tales of Vishnu

Lord Vishnu is known as the Preserver in the holy Hindu trinity along with Brahma, the Creator, and Shiva, the Destroyer. Whenever evil is on the rise, Vishnu descends onto the earth to uphold righteousness, preserve justice and annihilate sin.

Vishnu has countless incarnations, but the complete incarnations are ten in number and are called Dasha Avatar. These ten start with the form of a fish and work their way up to the human form, cast in the image of god.

The tales of these descents or avatars told in various Puranas have contributed in no small measure to make Vishnu one of the most popular Hindu deities. His worshippers are called Vaishnavas. Of the eighteen major Puranas, six are known as the Vaishnava Puranas as they eulogise Vishnu and depict him as the Supreme Self.

According to some scholars, the identification of Vishnu with Vasudeva-Krishna, the deified Yadava hero, contributed significantly to the rise of Vishnu as the greatest of the gods in the hierarchy of the Hindu pantheon. In fact, Vasudeva-Krishna came to be considered the eighth avatar of Vishnu.

Vishnu inspires more love than fear in his devotees. The Bhagawat Purana, from which the tales in this Amar Chitra Katha have been adapted, abounds in narratives of the benevolent acts of Vishnu. Although he is kind and sympathetic, he is never taken in by the apparent devotion of the wicked and wily. Even when they succeed in wresting favours from other deities, Vishnu maneuvers to bring about their destruction without falsifying the boons given to them by the gods.

**Script: Subba Rao**     **Illustrations: H.S. Chavan**     **Cover: C.M. Vitankar**

# GAJENDRA

INDRADYUMNA, THE PANDYAN KING, WAS FAMED FOR HIS VIRTUE.

ONE DAY, HE CALLED A MEETING OF HIS COUNSELLORS.

I HAVE DECIDED TO RETIRE TO THE FOREST AND DEVOTE ALL MY TIME TO THE WORSHIP OF THE LORD.

BUT, YOUR MAJESTY... THE KINGDOM...

DON'T TRY TO STOP ME. I AM CONFIDENT THAT YOU CAN AND WILL TAKE CARE OF THE KINGDOM.

INDRADYUMNA THEN RETIRED TO THE KULACHALA MOUNTAINS WHERE HE BUILT A COTTAGE FOR HIMSELF. OBSERVING THE VOW OF SILENCE, HE SAT WITH HIS MIND DWELLING UPON LORD VISHNU.

ONE DAY, SAGE AGASTYA CAME THAT WAY WITH HIS DISCIPLES.

WE HAVE COME TO HIS DOOR AND HE DOES NOT HAVE THE COURTESY TO WELCOME US!

YOUR ARROGANCE SHALL NOT GO UNPUNISHED! MAY YOU TURN INTO AN ELEPHANT.

IN HIS CELESTIAL ABODE, LORD VISHNU SMILED WHEN HE HEARD THE CURSE OF AGASTYA.

AGASTYA, YOU HAVE UNKNOWINGLY DONE MY DEVOTEE A GREAT SERVICE!

MEANWHILE, AT THE COTTAGE IN THE KULACHALA MOUNTAINS—

AS INDRADYUMNA BEGAN TO ROAM ABOUT IN THE FOREST, HE CAME ACROSS A HERD OF ELEPHANTS.

I WILL HAVE TO FIGHT THEIR KING. ONLY THEN WILL THE HERD ACCEPT ME.

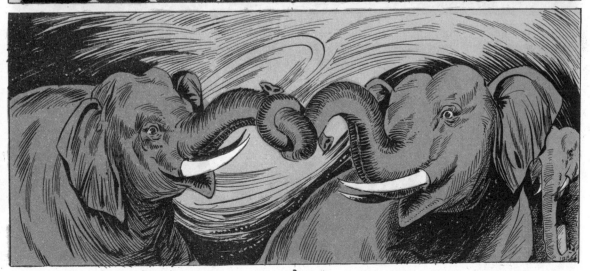

INDRADYUMNA EASILY OVERPOWERED HIS RIVAL.

WE SALUTE YOU, O GAJENDRA*!

ONE DAY —

LET US GO TO THE TRIKUTA MOUNTAIN. IT'S A BETTER PLACE THAN THIS.

WE'LL FOLLOW YOU TO THE END OF THE EARTH, O GAJENDRA.

LED BY GAJENDRA, THE HERD TOOK THE TRIKUTA FOREST BY STORM.

*KING ELEPHANT

THE ELEPHANTS THEN ENTERED A LAKE, WHICH WAS THE ABODE OF A CROCODILE.

HOW DARE THEY DISTURB MY SLUMBER!

THE FURIOUS CROCODILE BEGAN TO SWIM TOWARDS GAJENDRA.

I'LL TEACH THE KING ELEPHANT TO KEEP OUT OF MY LAKE!

MEANWHILE, AFTER THE REFRESHING BATH, AS THE ELEPHANTS BEGAN TO MOVE ON—

MY LEG! IT'S CAUGHT IN A TRAP...

IT'S A CROCODILE!

TRUMPETING LOUDLY, HE TRIED TO SHAKE OFF THE CROCODILE.

BUT ALL HIS EFFORTS WERE IN VAIN.

IT'S A CROCODILE. HE'S CAUGHT MY LEG.

WE'RE COMING, MY LORD. WE'LL SAVE YOU.

BUT THE HERD SOON HAD TO GIVE UP.

IT'S A PITY, BUT WE'LL HAVE TO DESERT OUR LEADER.

THE CROCODILE SEEMS TO HAVE DIVINE STRENGTH.

I CAN NO LONGER HOLD OUT.

GAJENDRA BECAME DESPERATE.

WHAT SHALL I DO?

O VISHNU, COME TO MY AID! YOU ARE MY ONLY REFUGE.

VISHNU HEARD THE PRAYER. MOUNTING GARUDA, HE LEFT HIS ABODE, VAIKUNTHA.

LORD, I BOW TO YOU. EMANCIPATE ME.

LORD VISHNU RESPONDED...

...AND THE CROCODILE FELL A VICTIM TO HIS DISCUS.

LORD!

OFFERING HIM THE LOTUS, GAJENDRA BOWED BEFORE VISHNU.

ARISE, GAJENDRA.

AT THE DIVINE TOUCH, GAJENDRA REGAINED HIS HUMAN FORM.

LORD, I WISH TO BEHOLD YOU ALL THE TIME. TAKE ME WITH YOU TO VAIKUNTHA.

SO BE IT.

# AMBARISHA

AFTER FASTING FOR THREE DAYS, KING AMBARISHA WORSHIPPED LORD VISHNU IN THE FOREST OF MADHUVANA ✱. HE WAS TO BREAK HIS FAST ON THE AUSPICIOUS DAY OF DWADASHI.✝

HAVING GIVEN AWAY ALMS···

···AND FED MENDICANTS···

✱THE FOREST REGION AROUND MATHURA ✝THE TWELFTH DAY OF THE FORTNIGHT

...HE HIMSELF WAS ABOUT TO BREAK HIS FAST WHEN SAGE DURVASA CAME BY.

ARISE, O KING.

HOLY ONE, YOU HAVE COME ON THE AUSPICIOUS DAY OF DWADASHI.

PLEASE BE MY GUEST AND BLESS ME.

I WILL. BUT FIRST LET ME BATHE IN THE HOLY YAMUNA.

DURVASA LEFT FOR THE RIVER.

HOURS PASSED BY.

THE HOLY ONE HAS BEEN AWAY A LONG WHILE. I ONLY HOPE HE RETURNS BEFORE NOON.

THE LEARNED MEN WHO HAD ASSEMBLED THERE, WERE WORRIED.

MY LORD, IF THE FAST IS NOT BROKEN BEFORE NOON, YOU WILL INCUR DEMERIT.

AND IF I DON'T WAIT FOR THE SAGE, I'LL INCUR HIS WRATH.

THIS IS A FINE PREDICAMENT, INDEED! WHAT SHALL I DO?

MY LORD, YOU COULD TAKE A SIP OF WATER AND BREAK THE FAST. THE SAGE WILL NOT BE OFFENDED BECAUSE YOU WILL EAT ONLY AFTER SERVING HIM.

WHAT YOU ADVISE SEEMS TO BE THE ONLY WAY OUT.

AS AMBARISHA POURED A LITTLE WATER INTO HIS PALM AND RAISED IT TO HIS LIPS—

AMBARISHA!

YOU ARE KNOWN TO BE A VIRTUOUS KING!

AND YET, YOU COULD NOT WAIT FOR YOUR GUEST!

HOLY SAGE, I HAVE ONLY TAKEN A SIP OF WATER. I HAD TO. OTHERWISE...

NOT A DROP OF WATER SHOULD HAVE BEEN DRUNK BEFORE FEEDING THE INVITED GUEST!

THE COURTIERS WERE AGHAST.

ISN'T THE SAGE AWARE OF THE CONDITIONS LAID DOWN FOR THE BREAKING OF THIS FAST?

WHY DID HE KEEP OUR KING WAITING?

DON'T WORRY. I THINK HE WILL SOON GET OVER HIS FIT OF RAGE.

BUT THE COURTIER WAS IN FOR A SHOCK. THE NEXT MOMENT—

YOU SHALL PAY FOR YOUR ARROGANCE, AMBARISHA!

THE SAGE TORE OFF A LOCK OF HIS MATTED HAIR.

AND LO! IT TURNED INTO A DISCUS.

AS IT CAME WHIRRING TOWARDS AMBARISHA—

ONLY LORD VISHNU CAN SAVE HIM NOW.

MEANWHILE—

GO, SUDARSHANA CHAKRA! GO TO THE RESCUE OF MY DEVOTEE!

LOOK! ANOTHER DISCUS!

IT'S LORD VISHNU'S SUDARSHANA CHAKRA!

HAVING DESTROYED THE DISCUS WHICH THREATENED AMBARISHA'S LIFE, SUDARSHANA CHAKRA FLEW TOWARDS DURVASA.

IT'S HEADING FOR ME!

THE SAGE BROKE INTO A RUN, PURSUED BY THE CHAKRA.

I AM BEING SCORCHED. I CANNOT BEAR IT.

AT LAST—

BRAHMA IS MY ONLY REFUGE.

HE CALLED ON BRAHMA.

LORD, PROTECT ME!

DURVASA, YOU HAVE INCURRED THE WRATH OF LORD VISHNU BY ATTEMPTING TO HARM HIS DEVOTEE.

NONE CAN PROTECT YOU NOW.

LORD SHIVA WON'T FAIL ME!

AT MOUNT KAILASA, THE ABODE OF SHIVA —

MY CHILD, SEEK HIS PROTECTION WHOSE ANGER YOU HAVE INVITED UPON YOURSELF.

DURVASA RUSHED TO LORD VISHNU.

O LORD! I HAVE OFFENDED YOUR DEVOTEE. PARDON ME! PROTECT ME!

O SAGE, HE WHO EMPLOYS HIS POWER TO INJURE THE VIRTUOUS, INVITES EVIL UPON HIMSELF.

ONLY AMBARISHA HAS THE POWER TO SAVE YOU. SEEK HIS PROTECTION.

DURVASA RETRACED HIS STEPS TO MADHUVANA.

AMBARISHA, TAKE PITY ON ME! CALL OFF THIS DISCUS!

AMBARISHA WAS MOVED BY DURVASA'S PLIGHT.

HAS THE GREAT SAGE BEEN REDUCED TO SUCH A PATHETIC STATE?

HE APPEALED TO SUDARSHANA CHAKRA.

IF LORD VISHNU HAS BEEN PLEASED WITH MY DEVOTION, LET SAGE DURVASA NO LONGER BE TROUBLED BY YOU.

AND THE SUDARSHANA CHAKRA DISAPPEARED.

THE NEXT MOMENT—

AMBARISHA, I AM GRATEFUL TO YOU. YOU HAVE RETURNED CRUELTY WITH KINDNESS.

THE DISCUS OF VISHNU WHICH COULD NOT BE CONTROLLED BY EITHER SHIVA OR BRAHMA, RESPECTS YOUR WORDS. WHAT IS THE SECRET OF YOUR POWER?

THE LOVE OF LORD VISHNU.

THUS DID VISHNU DEMONSTRATE HIS LOVE FOR HIS DEVOTEES.

# VRIKASURA

THE FOOLISH BUT MIGHTY ASURA, VRIKA, ONCE DECIDED TO PROPITIATE LORD SHIVA.

HE CUT OFF HIS FLESH AND OFFERED IT TO THE LORD.

LORD, WITH THIS OFFERING, MAY YOU APPEAR BEFORE ME.

HE DOES NOT APPEAR. PERHAPS IT IS ONLY THE OFFERING OF MY HEAD THAT WILL PROPITIATE THE LORD.

WHEN HE WAS ABOUT TO SEVER HIS HEAD FROM THE BODY—

STOP, VRIKA! THERE IS NO NEED TO KILL YOUR-SELF TO PLEASE ONE WHO IS SATISFIED WITH A MERE OFFER-ING OF WATER.

WHAT IS THE BOON YOU SEEK?

I WISH TO CONQUER THE WORLD. MAY ANYONE ON WHOSE HEAD I LAY MY PALM, DIE.

SO BE IT.

22

23

MEANWHILE, AS VRIKA RAN IN SEARCH OF SHIVA, A YOUNG BRAHMACHARI *MET HIM.

WHERE ARE YOU RUNNING TO? WHOM ARE YOU SEEKING? REST FOR A WHILE. YOU SEEM TIRED.

VRIKA TOLD HIM OF SHIVA'S BOON.

WHEN I WANTED TO TRY IT ON HIM, HE RAN AWAY.

THAT'S BECAUSE THE MOMENT YOU PLACED YOUR PALM ON HIS HEAD, YOU WOULD REALISE THAT HE HAD DUPED YOU.

WHAT! SHIVA DUPING A DEVOTEE! I CAN'T BELIEVE IT.

THEN WHY DON'T YOU PLACE YOUR PALM ON YOUR OWN HEAD AND SEE?

A GOOD IDEA!

*CELIBATE

WITHOUT STOPPING TO THINK, THE FOOLISH ASURA PLACED HIS PALM ON HIS HEAD.

THE NEXT MOMENT, HE FELL DEAD. THE CLEVER BRAHMACHARI WAS NONE OTHER THAN VISHNU.

JUST THEN, SHIVA APPEARED.

I AM SORRY THAT THE UNFORTUNATE ASURA HAD TO DIE.

IT WAS INEVITABLE. HE WHO SECURES A BOON TO DESTROY OTHERS SEEKS HIS OWN DESTRUCTION.

# RANTIDEVA

ONCE BRAHMA, INDRA AND THE OTHER DEVAS CALLED ON LORD VISHNU.

LORD, WHO DO YOU CONSIDER YOUR GREATEST DEVOTEE?

RANTIDEVA.

THAT KING? JUST BECAUSE HE HAS GIVEN UP HIS KINGDOM AND FASTED FOR FORTY-EIGHT DAYS?

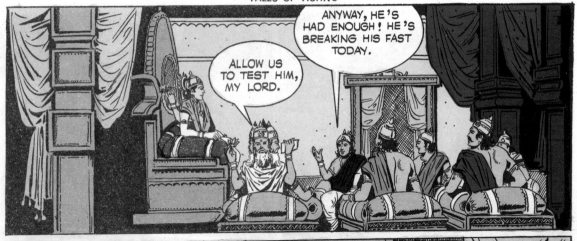

* GOD'S GIFT

HOLY ONE, I AM HUNGRY. GIVE ME SOMETHING TO EAT.

MAY THE LORD BE PLEASED! TAKE HALF OF WHAT IS MINE.

MAY GOD BLESS YOU.

AS THE BRAHMAN WENT AWAY, A FARMER CAME ALONG.

HOLY ONE, I AM DYING OF HUNGER.

YOU SHALL SHARE WHAT I HAVE.

AS RANTIDEVA WAS ABOUT TO EAT WHAT WAS LEFT—

MASTER, DO YOU HAVE SOMETHING FOR ME AND MY POOR DOGS?

WHAT LITTLE I HAVE, IS YOURS.

WHILE THE BEGGAR AND HIS DOGS ATE —

A STRANGE PEACE FILLS MY HEART.

LATER, THE DEVA* WHO HAD CALLED ON RANTIDEVA IN THE GUISE OF THE BEGGAR, JOINED THE OTHERS.

HE GAVE ME ALL THE FOOD HE HAD.

SHOULD WE ADMIT DEFEAT, THEN?

NOT YET.

IT WAS YAMA THE LORD OF DEATH.

MEANWHILE —

GLORY TO THE LORD. I WAS ABLE TO SERVE HIM BY FEEDING THE HUNGRY. LET ME HAVE SOME WATER AND BREAK MY FAST.

MASTER!

CELESTIAL BEING

29

* EMANCIPATION OF THE SOUL

THE NEXT MOMENT, VISHNU AND THE OTHER DEVAS APPEARED BEFORE RANTIDEVA.

# Classic Collections

The immortal tales of Amar Chitra Katha
are now available as 3-in-I digests with a special
selection of three delightful tales in one comic book.

Tales from the Panchatantra

Tales of Birbal

More Tales of Birbal

Great Plays of Kalidasa

Great Sanskrit Plays

Great Indian Emperors

Vishnu the Saviour

Ranas of Mewar

Matchless Wits

More Tales from the Jatakas

Vishnu to the Rescue

Buddhist Tales

More Buddhist Tales

Tales told by Sri Ramakrishna

Further Tales from the Jatakas

The Sons of the Pandavas

**Each 96-page digest is now available at a special online price of
Rs 68 (MRP Rs 80) at www.AmarChitraKatha.com. Start your collection today!**

## INDIA BOOK HOUSE

Mahalaxmi Chambers, 5th Floor, 22 Bhulabhai Desai Road, Mumbai 400 026, India.
Tel.: 2352 3409, 2352 5636  Fax: 2353 8406  E-mail: info@amarchitrakath.com

# Tales of Narada

Illustrated Classics From India

# Tales of Narada

The divine sage Narada is one of the most popular figures in Puranic lore. No event of significance takes place in the Puranas without the presence or the overt participation of Narada. He is most often depicted as a messenger, always on the move, visiting the devas (gods), the manavas (humans) and the asuras (demons) in turn, and being honoured by all. He is a great devotee of Lord Vishnu.

Although Narada is always referred to with respect in mythological tales, he is often misunderstood and ridiculed by the common people as a carrier of tales and a mischief-maker. But his 'mischief' invariably brings about the downfall of the wicked and the triumph of good.

Narada is credited with the invention of the veena (a musical instrument), the authorship of a code of law and of the Narada Bhakti Sutra (aphorisms on devotion).

The three tales included in this Amar Chitra Katha are based on the Shiva Purana and some popular legends. These stories tell us how Narada, although a divine sage, often fell prey to temptation and pride and became conceited. Fortunately for him, every time he succumbed to human weaknesses, Vishnu was beside him to pull him through. Eventually, he became free from human failings and attained true equanimity of the mind.

**Script: Onkar Nath Sharma        Illustrations: P.B. Kavadi        Cover: C.M. Vitankar**

# NARADA CONQUERS TEMPTATION

NARADA WAS A DEVARSHI* WHO WAS ALWAYS TRAVELLING ROUND THE WORLD, OFFERING GUIDANCE TO THE DEVOTEES OF THE LORD.

AFTER HAVING GAINED TRUE KNOWLEDGE FROM HIS FATHER, BRAHMA...

...HE TOOK THE VOW OF CELIBACY.

I SHALL NOT MARRY. I WILL SERVE LORD NARAYANA.+

* CELESTIAL SAGE  + VISHNU

NARADA PRACTISED SEVERE AUSTERITIES IN THE HIMALAYAS.

INDRA, KING OF THE DEVAS, BECAME SUSPICIOUS OF NARADA'S MOTIVES. HE SPOKE TO BRIHASPATI * ABOUT IT.

I WONDER WHAT HE IS AFTER.

IT COULD BE YOUR THRONE.

WHAT SHALL I DO? AH! I COULD TEMPT HIM WITH WORLDLY PLEASURES AND MAKE HIM SWERVE FROM HIS PATH.

WITH THIS IN MIND, INDRA SENT FOR KAMADEVA.**

KAMA, I NEED YOUR HELP. YOU MUST MAKE NARADA GIVE UP HIS AUSTERITIES.

I'LL TRY, MY LORD.

*THE ROYAL PRECEPTOR OF THE DEVAS ** THE GOD OF LOVE

KAMA CAME TO THE COLD, BARREN SPOT WHERE NARADA WAS SITTING, DEEP IN MEDITATION.

AS HE SHOT THE FIRST ARROW...

...THE SCENE SUDDENLY CHANGED...

...AND A BEAUTIFUL APSARA* APPEARED BEFORE NARADA.

* CELESTIAL DAMSEL

SHE BEGAN TO DANCE BEFORE HIM.

BUT NARADA'S EYES WERE CLOSED TO HER CHARMS.

O SAGE, OPEN YOUR EYES AND BEHOLD YOUR SLAVE.

BUT NARADA HARDLY HEARD HER.

REALISING, THAT SHE WOULD NEVER SUCCEED IN DISTRACTING THE SAGE, THE APSARA LEFT FOR HER HEAVENLY ABODE.

KAMA HAD TO ACKNOWLEDGE DEFEAT.

YOU ARE A GREAT ASCETIC, O SUPREME SAGE! I HAVE FAILED. I BEG TO BE FORGIVEN FOR MY AUDACITY.

NARADA OPENED HIS EYES.

OH, KAMA! WHO SENT YOU HERE?

WHO BUT LORD INDRA!

GO AND TELL INDRA THAT NARADA HAS CONQUERED ALL DESIRES, THAT HE IS ABOVE TEMPTATION.

AND NARADA GLOATED OVER HIS ACHIEVEMENT.

I HAVE DEFEATED KAMA! LORD SHIVA IS NO LONGER THE ONLY CONQUEROR OF THIS INVINCIBLE GOD.*

I MUST GO AND TELL SHIVA ABOUT IT. HE MUST NOW ACCEPT ME AS HIS EQUAL.

*SEE AMAR CHITRA KATHA NO. 29 — SHIVA PARVATI

AT KAILAS, THE ABODE OF SHIVA —

SALUTATIONS TO LORD SHIVA!

COME, NARADA! YOU SEEM PLEASED. WHAT'S THE REASON?

I HAVE CONQUERED KAMADEVA! INDRA SENT HIM TO TEMPT ME. BUT KAMA FAILED!

I AM GLAD TO KNOW THAT! BUT KEEP THE MATTER TO YOURSELF. IN ANY CASE, NEVER BRAG ABOUT IT TO LORD VISHNU!

SHIVA IS JEALOUS OF ME. WHY SHOULDN'T I SPEAK ABOUT MY SUCCESS TO VISHNU? VISHNU, WHO LOVES ME SO DEARLY! I AM SURE HE WILL BE PROUD TO HEAR OF MY VICTORY OVER KAMA.

6

HE WENT STRAIGHT TO VISHNU'S ABODE.

MAY I PAY MY RESPECTS TO THE GREAT LORD?

COME, NARADA! I AM SO GLAD TO SEE YOU.

YOU WILL BE MORE SO, MY LORD, WHEN YOU LEARN THAT I, YOUR DEVOTEE, HAVE CONQUERED KAMADEVA.

IS THAT SO?

YES, MY LORD! SHIVA IS NO LONGER THE ONLY CONQUEROR OF KAMA. I, YOUR DEVOTEE, AM ABOVE TEMPTATION TOO.

BUT NEVER CEASE TO BE ON YOUR GUARD. YOU NEVER KNOW...

HUH! VISHNU DIDN'T SEEM TOO PLEASED ABOUT MY ACHIEVEMENT EITHER. I AM NO WEAKLING! DOESN'T HE KNOW THAT? WHY SHOULD HE WARN ME TO BE ON MY GUARD?

AS NARADA MOVED ON, SUDDENLY—

WHAT'S THAT? WHAT A WONDERFUL CITY! I'VE NEVER SEEN ONE LIKE IT BEFORE! I MUST VISIT IT.

WHEN HE REACHED THE CITY—

WHO IS THE RULER OF THIS BIG AND CHARMING CITY?

DON'T YOU KNOW? IT BELONGS TO THE GLORIOUS KING, SHEELA-NIDHI. YOU'LL FIND HIM IN HIS PALACE.

HEARING THAT NARADA HAD COME TO VISIT HIM, THE KING CAME OUT TO RECEIVE HIM.

WELCOME, O SAGE! YOU DO US GREAT HONOUR.

JUST THEN THE PRINCESS CAME ON THE SCENE.

THIS IS MY DAUGHTER, SHRIMATI.

WHAT A BEAUTIFUL MAIDEN SHE IS!

AS WAS THE CUSTOM, SHRIMATI BOWED TO THE SAGE.

ARISE, DEAR CHILD. MAY YOU EVER BE HAPPY.

SHE IS READY FOR MARRIAGE. I PLAN TO HOLD A SWAYAMVARA FOR HER SOON.

NARADA GAZED AT THE PRINCESS.

YOUR DAUGHTER IS GODDESS LAXMI*INCARNATE. ONE NO LESS THAN HARI⊕IN GLORY AND POWER, SHALL BE HER HUSBAND.

* THE GODDESS OF FORTUNE, VISHNU'S CONSORT ⊕VISHNU

YOUR WORDS FILL OUR HEARTS WITH JOY. I CANNOT WAIT TO ANNOUNCE THE DATE OF HER SWAYAMVARA.

IF I CAN GET THIS PRINCESS FOR A WIFE, THERE WILL BE NONE MORE FORTUNATE AND POWERFUL IN ALL THE UNIVERSE. BUT HOW SHALL I WIN HER?

NARADA PRAYED FERVENTLY TO LORD VISHNU.

AT LAST, WHEN LORD VISHNU APPEARED BEFORE HIM —

LORD, LET MY FACE RESEMBLE HARI'S.*

YOU SHALL CERTAINLY HAVE THE FACE OF HARI.

BUT NOT THE HARI YOU'RE THINKING OF.

* ANOTHER NAME FOR VISHNU

WHEN NARADA MADE HIS REQUEST HE HAD FORGOTTEN THAT THE WORD HARI ALSO MEANT A MONKEY! AND HE COULD NOT SEE HIS OWN FACE.

HE WENT TO THE SWAYAMVARA HALL FULL OF CONFIDENCE, SURE OF HIS VICTORY.

WHO COULD THAT STRANGE CREATURE BE? A MAN WITH A MONKEY'S FACE! HA! HA!

AND WHAT DOES HE WANT HERE? THE HEART OF SHRIMATI, THE MOST BEAUTIFUL PRINCESS IN THE WORLD?

I HAVE THE HONOUR OF WELCOMING YOU, OUR ROYAL GUESTS, TO THE SWAYAMVARA OF MY DAUGHTER SHRIMATI. SHE SHALL CHOOSE ONE AMONG YOU AS HER HUSBAND. COME MY DAUGHTER, MAKE YOUR CHOICE!

HARDLY NOTICING HIM, SHRIMATI WALKED ON.

12

THE NEXT MOMENT—

OH! MY LORD!

AH! THERE HE IS! LORD, WHY DID YOU···

BEFORE HE COULD COMPLETE HIS QUESTION, SHRIMATI HAD GARLANDED VISHNU.

SO THAT WAS IT! HE WANTED HER FOR HIMSELF. THE TRAITOR!

HE CHARGED FORWARD IN A RAGE.

YOU PROMISED TO GIVE ME YOUR FACE AND GAVE ME A MONKEY'S INSTEAD! WHY?

MY DEAR NARADA, YOU ARE A SCHOLAR OF SANSKRIT. DON'T YOU KNOW, HARI ALSO MEANS MONKEY? YOU DIDN'T SPECIFY WHICH HARI YOU MEANT.

17

NARAYANA, NARAYANA!

WHERE DO YOU COME FROM? WHAT CAN I DO FOR YOU?

WE WERE ON OUR WAY TO THE CITY. IT'LL SOON BE DARK AND THE FOREST IS INFESTED WITH WILD ANIMALS. WE SEEK SHELTER FOR A NIGHT.

YOU ARE WELCOME TO STAY WITH ME, MY FRIENDS, AND PARTAKE OF WHAT MEAGRE FARE I CAN OFFER YOU.

I AM GRATEFUL TO GOD FOR GIVING ME THIS OPPORTUNITY TO SERVE HIM. PRAISED BE HIS NAME!

THERE ARE TWO GUESTS IN THE HOUSE. PLEASE MAKE SOME EXTRA CHAPATIS.*

*UNLEAVENED BREAD

THIS IS ALL THE FLOUR I HAVE, AND THE CHILDREN ARE CLAMOURING FOR MORE FOOD.

NEVER MIND! THE GUESTS MUST HAVE THEIR FILL. MAKE SOME GRUEL FOR THE CHILDREN.

SOON AFTER THEY HAD FINISHED EATING THE CHAPATIS —

HOW CAN THIS SIMPLE HOUSE-HOLDER BE SUCH A GREAT DEVOTEE.

I AM STILL VERY HUNGRY.

THE FARMER WENT TO THE KITCHEN.

IS THERE ANY FOOD LEFT?

NOTHING, EXCEPT THE GRUEL I COOKED FOR THE CHILDREN.

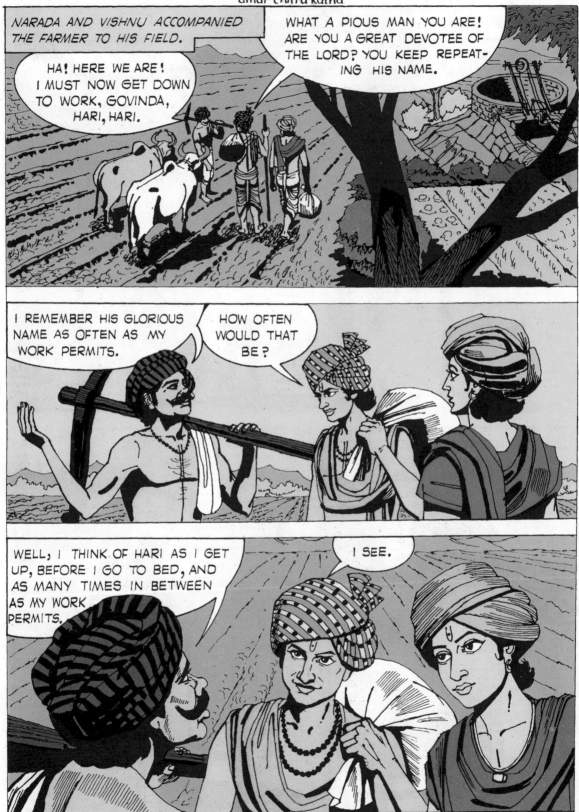

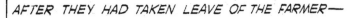

AFTER THEY HAD TAKEN LEAVE OF THE FARMER—

HE THINKS OF YOU AT NIGHT, IN THE MORNING AND A FEW TIMES IN BETWEEN. WHILE I THINK OF YOU ALL THE TIME. AND YET YOU CALL HIM ONE OF YOUR GREATEST DEVOTEES!

YOU'LL SOON SEE WHY, DEAR NARADA.

VISHNU GAVE NARADA A VESSEL FILLED TO THE BRIM WITH OIL.

BALANCE THIS VESSEL ON YOUR HEAD, WALK ROUND THAT HILL AND COME BACK HERE WITHOUT SPILLING A DROP OF THE OIL.

IT WON'T BE EASY, BUT WITH YOUR GRACE IS THERE ANYTHING THAT CANNOT BE ACCOMPLISHED?

AND NARADA SET OFF.

I MUST BE CAUTIOUS LEST THE OIL SHOULD SPILL.

AH! AH! THAT WAS A CLOSE CALL! HAD I SLIPPED, THE OIL WOULD HAVE SPILT. I MUST BE MORE CAREFUL.

WHEN NARADA SUCCESSFULLY COMPLETED THE ROUND—

YOU'RE BACK. GOOD! BUT TELL ME HOW MANY TIMES DID YOU REMEMBER ME DURING THE WALK?

NOT ONCE, I'M AFRAID. HOW COULD I? ALL MY ATTENTION WAS FIXED ON THE OIL AND THE VESSEL!

THAT FARMER HAS HARD WORK TO DO. YET HE REMEMBERS ME — AT LEAST A FEW TIMES. WHILE YOU COULD NOT REMEMBER ME EVEN ONCE!

I CONCEDE IT, MY LORD. THOSE WHO REMEMBER YOU AMIDST WORLDLY CARES ARE WITHOUT DOUBT YOUR GREATEST DEVOTEES.

# NARADA ENLIGHTENED

THE CELESTIAL SAGE, NARADA, ONCE CAME TO DWARAKA, TO SEE LORD KRISHNA.

WELCOME, NARADA. WHAT BRINGS YOU HERE?

KRISHNA, I WANT TO KNOW WHAT MAYA* IS? CAN YOU EXPLAIN?

NARADA, MAYA CAN'T BE EXPLAINED. IT HAS TO BE EXPERIENCED, TO BE UNDERSTOOD. COME WITH ME.

BOTH KRISHNA AND NARADA LEFT DWARAKA...

* ILLUSION

25

···AND KEPT WALKING TILL THEY CAME TO A DESERT.

WHERE ARE WE GOING? HOW CAN I EXPERIENCE MAYA IN A DESERT, KRISHNA?

BE PATIENT, NARADA.

AFTER THEY HAD WALKED A GOOD DISTANCE, KRISHNA SUDDENLY STOPPED.

I CAN'T WALK ANY FURTHER, NARADA. MY THROAT IS PARCHED. TAKE THIS···AND FETCH ME···SOME··· WATER.

HOLD ON, KRISHNA. I'LL BE BACK SOON.

NARADA WENT IN SEARCH OF WATER.

IT LOOKS LIKE A SETTLEMENT THERE.

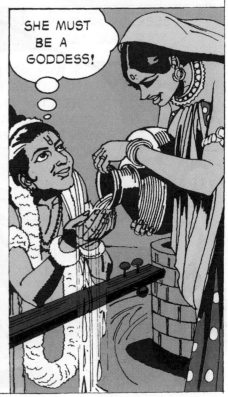

NARADA FOLLOWED THE DAMSEL···

···TO HER HOUSE.

ARE YOU THE MASTER OF THIS HOUSE?

NOT ONLY OF THIS HOUSE BUT ALSO OF THE ENTIRE VILLAGE. WHAT DO YOU WANT, STRANGER?

I SEEK THE HAND OF YOUR DAUGHTER.

WHY NOT? YOU LOOK YOUNG, HEALTHY AND STRONG. BUT··· THE MAN WHO MARRIES MY DAUGHTER MUST STAY IN THIS VILLAGE, IN THIS HOUSE.

IS THAT ALL? I'M WILLING TO ABIDE BY YOUR CONDITION.

ANYTHING TO MAKE THAT GIRL MY WIFE.

THE MARRIAGE SOON TOOK PLACE.

SOON AFTER THE MARRIAGE, THE OLD CHIEFTAIN DIED. NARADA HAD TO ASSUME HIS TITLE AND HIS RESPONSIBILITIES.

I WANT THE WORK FINISHED BY EVENING.

IT WILL BE DONE, MASTER.

NARADA WAS BLESSED WITH FOUR CHILDREN.

FATHER, PUT HIM DOWN AND CARRY ME.

WHEN NARADA WAS AT THE PEAK OF HIS SUCCESS, DISASTER CAME IN THE FORM OF CYCLONIC WINDS, RAIN AND FLOODS.

THE HOUSE WILL SOON BE SUBMERGED! WHAT SHALL WE DO?

FATHER!

NARADA PUT HIS FAMILY INTO A BOAT AND TRIED TO KEEP AFLOAT, ON THE SWIRLING WATERS.

BUT THE BOAT CAPSIZED. NARADA TRIED IN VAIN TO SAVE HIS WIFE AND CHILDREN.

FATHER!

WHERE ARE YOU! DON'T PANIC. I AM COMING!

FATHER!

A HUGE WAVE THREW NARADA ON TO THE SHORE.

MY WIFE GONE! MY CHILDREN DROWNED! HOW CAN I LIVE WITHOUT THEM?

SUDDENLY, HE HEARD A VOICE.

NARADA, I AM THIRSTY. WHERE IS THE WATER?

NARADA TURNED AND BEHELD KRISHNA.

KRISHNA! MY WIFE! MY CHILDREN! BRING THEM BACK TO LIFE.

COME TO YOUR SENSES, NARADA. THERE NEVER WAS ANY WIFE OR CHILDREN. IT WAS ALL MAYA.

I AM GRATEFUL TO YOU FOR ENLIGHTENING ME, KRISHNA. LIFE ITSELF IS AN ILLUSION FROM WHICH IT IS DIFFICULT TO ESCAPE. ONLY WITH YOUR GRACE CAN THIS ILLUSION BE CONQUERED!

31

# Timeless Treasures

The legendary sagas of Amar Chitra Katha are now available as 5-in-1 digests with a distinctive compilation of five enthralling tales in one comic book.

| | |
|---|---|
| Stories of Birbal | Great Rulers of India |
| Stories from the Jatakas | Brave Rajputs |
| Stories from the Panchatantra | Ancient Tales of Wit and Wisdom |
| Stories of Rama | Further Stories from the Jatakas |
| More Stories from the Jatakas | Stories from the Bhagawat |
| Devotees of Vishnu | Stories of Buddha |
| Heroes from the Mahabharata | Stories from the Mahabharata |
| Stories from Sanskrit Drama | Great Freedom Fighters |

**Each 160-page digest is now available at a special online price of Rs 175 (MRP Rs 195) at www.AmarChitraKatha.com. Start your collection today!**

**INDIA BOOK HOUSE**

Mahalaxmi Chambers, 5th Floor, 22 Bhulabhai Desai Road, Mumbai 400 026, India.
Tel.: 2352 3409, 2352 5636  Fax: 2353 8406  E-mail: info@amarchitrakath.com

AMAR
CHITRA
KATHA

# Prahlad

Illustrated Classics From India

# Prahlad

When the sons of Brahma came to the gates of Vishnu's abode, the gate-keepers, Jaya and Vijaya, did not know who they were and refused them entry. Enraged, the sons of Brahma cursed them, "You shall be born three times on earth. In each of the births you shall be slain by Vishnu or his incarnation. Only then shall you regain your place in Heaven."

Jaya and Vijaya were born upon earth first as the asura brothers, Hiranyaksha and Hiranyakashipu; then as the rakshasas, Ravana and Kumbhakarna; and lastly as the evil kshatriyas, Shishupala and Dantavakra.

As per the divine prophecy, Hiranyaksha was slain by Vishnu during Vishnu's incarnation of the boar (Varaha). Hiranyakashipu hated Vishnu for having killed his brother. But his son Prahlad was an ardent devotee of Vishnu. Hiranyakashipu tried by various methods to sway the mind of his son, coaxing, threatening and persecuting him in turn. But his efforts were in vain. Ultimately, the evil Hiranyakashipu brought about his own destruction, and Lord Vishnu himself rewarded Prahlad's unerring devotion.

The story given in this book is based on the Bhagawat Purana and the Vishnu Purana.

Script: Kamala Chandrakant     Illustrations: Souren Roy     Cover: P.D. Chopra

# PRAHLAD

PRAHLAD WAS THE SON OF THE ASURA, HIRANYAKASHIPU.

HIRANYAKASHIPU'S BROTHER HIRANYAKSHA HAD BEEN SLAIN BY VISHNU.

O BROTHER ASURAS! I SHALL DESTROY VISHNU AND KEEP THE OTHER GODS IN HEAVEN SUBDUED.

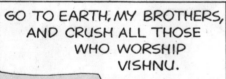

GO TO EARTH, MY BROTHERS, AND CRUSH ALL THOSE WHO WORSHIP VISHNU.

THE ASURAS, BY NATURE FOND OF OPPRESSING OTHERS, JOYFULLY OBEYED THE COMMAND.

WHILE THE ASURAS WERE BUSY HARASSING THE DEVOTEES OF VISHNU, THE GODS WENT ABOUT PROTECTING THEM.

THE ASURAS RETURNED TO HIRANYAKASHIPU.

LORD! WE CANNOT CARRY OUT YOUR ORDERS. THE SERVANTS OF VISHNU THWART OUR EFFORTS.

I WILL HAVE TO MATCH MY POWERS TO VISHNU'S TO LORD OVER THE THREE WORLDS!

SO HE BEGAN TO PERFORM SEVERE PENANCES.

WHEN THE GODS FOUND THAT VISHNU'S DEVOTEES NO LONGER NEEDED THEIR PROTECTION THEY RETURNED TO THEIR HEAVENLY ABODE.

THERE THEY HELD COUNCIL.

YES! THIS IS THE MOMENT. THE ASURA KING IS AWAY, DEEP IN HIS PENANCE. LET US ATTACK HIS PEOPLE AND VANQUISH THEM FOREVER.

THE ASURAS WERE PANIC-STRICKEN.

THE GODS ARE PLANNING TO ATTACK US. WITHOUT OUR LORD WE ARE HELPLESS.

FLEE!

FLEE!

IN THEIR HASTE AND ANXIETY TO SAVE THEIR OWN LIVES, THEY DID NOT BOTHER TO TAKE EVEN THEIR WIVES, CATTLE OR MONEY.

WAIT!

DO NOT LEAVE US BEHIND!

THE GODS RANSACKED THE ASURA CITY AND DESTROYED HIRANYA-KASHIPU'S PALACE.

AH! I HAVE THE GREATEST BOOTY OF THE ASURAS - HIRANYAKASHIPU'S QUEEN.

WHILE INDRA WAS TRANSPORTING HER TO HEAVEN, HE MET SAGE NARADA.

WAIT! YOU SHOULD NOT CARRY OFF THIS GUILTLESS QUEEN, THE CHASTE WIFE OF ANOTHER.

SHE IS GOING TO BE THE MOTHER OF HIRANYA-KASHIPU'S SON. SHE SHALL BE WITH ME TILL THE CHILD IS BORN!

ONCE THE CHILD IS BORN AND I HAVE SLAIN IT, I SHALL LET HER GO.

BUT THE CHILD, PRAHLAD, IN HER, IS NOT LIKE THE FATHER. HE IS DESTINED TO BE DIFFERENT AND GREAT.

BESIDES HE WILL BE A DEVOTEE OF VISHNU AND IS NOT DESTINED TO DIE AT YOUR HANDS.

I ACCEPT YOUR WORDS O HONOURED SAGE. HIRANYAKASHIPU'S QUEEN IS FREE TO GO WHERE SHE PLEASES.

INDRA WENT BACK TO HEAVEN AND SAGE NARADA TOOK HIRANYA-KASHIPU'S WIFE TO HIS OWN HERMITAGE.

MY DEAR DAUGHTER, YOU MAY LIVE HERE TILL YOUR HUSBAND COMES FOR YOU.

SHE LIVED IN THE ASHRAM OF THE GREAT SAGE AND LEARNED ABOUT RELIGION AND THE GLORY OF VISHNU FROM HIM. THE CHILD WITHIN HER, PRAHLAD, TOO, ABSORBED ALL THIS KNOWLEDGE.

VISHNU IS THE SOUL OF ALL CREATED THINGS AND IS PRESENT EVERYWHERE.

IN THE MEANWHILE, WHEN INDRA REACHED HEAVEN—

WHAT'S THE MATTER?

HIRANYAKASHIPU'S AUSTERITIES ARE SCORCHING THE THREE WORLDS.

QUICK! LET US GO TO BRAHMA, OUR CREATOR.

WHEN THEY REACHED THE ABODE OF BRAHMA—

O GREAT ONE, PACIFY HIRANYA-KASHIPU BEFORE HE DESTROYS ALL.

BE CALM, MY SONS. I SHALL SEE WHAT I CAN DO.

THE MIGHTY BRAHMA, ACCOMPANIED BY HIS CELESTIAL SAGES, WENT TO HIRANYAKASHIPU'S HERMITAGE.

BRAHMA WAS ASTONISHED BY THE SIGHT.

ARISE HIRANYA-KASHIPU. ANY BOON THAT YOU ASK OF ME SHALL BE YOURS.

AS SOON AS THE DROPS OF BRAHMA'S HOLY WATER TOUCHED HIM, HIRANYAKASHIPU CAME OUT OF HIS TRANCE AND SALUTED BRAHMA.

IF SO, THEN I PRAY THAT MY DEATH BE NOT CAUSED BY MAN OR BEAST, WITH A WEAPON OR WITHOUT, DURING DAY OR NIGHT, INDOORS OR OUTDOORS, ON EARTH OR IN THE SKY. GRANT ME THE UNDISPUTED LORDSHIP OVER THE MATERIAL WORLD.

MY SON! THE BOONS YOU HAVE ASKED OF ME ARE OBTAINED WITH GREAT DIFFICULTY. YET I GRANT THEM TO YOU.

BRAHMA DEPARTED AND HIRANYAKASHIPU WAS OVERJOYED.

HIRANYAKASHIPU BROUGHT HIS WIFE BACK TO THEIR CITY WHERE PRAHLAD WAS BORN.

MY SUCCESSOR! YOU SHALL VANQUISH THE GODS.

HIRANYAKASHIPU, WITH HIS NEW POWERS, RENEWED HIS HOSTILITIES AGAINST VISHNU AND HIS FOLLOWERS.

HE DROVE THE GODS OUT OF THEIR ABODE AND ESTABLISHED HIMSELF IN HEAVEN.

THERE IS NONE STRONGER THAN I. I AM THE LORD OF THE THREE WORLDS. I SHALL BE WORSHIPPED AS SUCH!

ALL THE GODS IN HEAVEN EXCEPT BRAHMA, VISHNU AND SHIVA, BEGAN TO WORSHIP THE INTOXICATED HIRANYAKASHIPU.

GOOD! YOU ARE WISE TO WORSHIP ME; OR IS IT FEAR THAT I MIGHT SLAY YOU OTHERWISE?

AT LAST THE OPPRESSED GODS AND DEVOTEES OF VISHNU APPEALED TO HIM.

O LORD, WE SHALL FOREGO SLEEP AND LIVE ONLY ON AIR TILL YOU COME TO OUR AID.

AFTER A FEW DAYS_

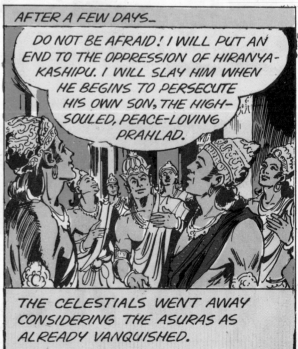

DO NOT BE AFRAID! I WILL PUT AN END TO THE OPPRESSION OF HIRANYA-KASHIPU. I WILL SLAY HIM WHEN HE BEGINS TO PERSECUTE HIS OWN SON, THE HIGH-SOULED, PEACE-LOVING PRAHLAD.

THE CELESTIALS WENT AWAY CONSIDERING THE ASURAS AS ALREADY VANQUISHED.

PRAHLAD IN THE MEANWHILE WAS GROWING UP AND WAS HIRANYAKASHIPU'S DELIGHT. ONE DAY—

DEAR SON! TELL ME. WHAT DO YOU THINK IS THE BEST THING IN LIFE?

TO RENOUNCE THE WORLD AND SEEK REFUGE IN VISHNU.

HIRANYAKASHIPU LAUGHED. THEN HE CALLED HIS SON'S TEACHER TO HIM.

GUARD HIM CLOSELY. I THINK THAT THE FOLLOWERS OF VISHNU ARE SECRETLY INFLUENCING HIM. DON'T LET HIM OUT OF YOUR SIGHT.

PRAHLAD WENT TO LIVE IN THE HOUSE OF HIS TEACHER.

O PRAHLAD! TELL ME THE TRUTH. DO NOT BE AFRAID. WHO HAS SPOKEN TO YOU ABOUT VISHNU?

WHO BUT VISHNU HIMSELF. HE FILLS ME WITH THE KNOWLEDGE.

HIS TEACHER WAS FURIOUS.

WHERE IS THE CANE? THIS BOY MUST BE SEVERELY PUNISHED.

THIS WILL TEACH YOU NOT TO PRAISE VISHNU, THE SWORN ENEMY OF OUR PEOPLE.

AND SO THE DAYS PASSED.

I THINK YOU ARE NOW READY TO MEET YOUR FATHER.

THE TEACHER THEN SENT FOR PRAHLAD'S MOTHER.

ANOINT HIM WITH PERFUMES AND DECORATE HIM WITH ORNAMENTS. WE WISH TO PRESENT HIM BEFORE LORD HIRANYA-KASHIPU.

THE BEDECKED PRAHLAD WAS THEN LED TO HIRANYAKASHIPU.

O MY SON! MAY YOU LIVE LONG.

THUS COMMANDED BY HIRANYAKASHIPU, THE ASURAS BEGAN TO ATTACK PRAHLAD.

BUT THEIR STROKES WERE OF NO AVAIL FOR PRAHLAD WAS DEEPLY ENGROSSED IN HIS ADORATION OF VISHNU.

HIRANYAKASHIPU HAD THE MOST DEADLY SERPENTS BROUGHT. THEY WERE LET LOOSE ON PRAHLAD. BUT THEIR FANGS TURNED IMPOTENT.

HIRANYAKASHIPU THEN CALLED FOR MIGHTY ELEPHANTS AND MADE THEM TRAMPLE UPON PRAHLAD. BUT ONCE AGAIN IT WAS THE ELEPHANTS THAT WERE INJURED.

THEN HIRANYAKASHIPU HAD HIM PUSHED OFF A CLIFF AND...

...THROWN INTO A BLAZING FIRE.

BUT NOT A HAIR ON PRAHLAD'S HEAD WAS SINGED.

IN DESPERATION HIRANYAKASHIPU HAD HIM FED WITH A DEADLY POISON BUT IT TURNED INTO NECTAR IN PRAHLAD'S MOUTH.

INCREDIBLE! HAS DEATH NO STING FOR HIM?

HE IS IMMORTAL AND FEARS NOTHING.

WILL **HE** BE THE CAUSE OF MY DEATH?

AS HIRANYAKASHIPU SAT BROODING, PRAHLAD'S TEACHER CAME TO SEE HIM.

WE'LL TRY AGAIN, MY LORD!

ALL RIGHT! TAKE THE BOY BACK AND SEE WHAT YOU CAN DO.

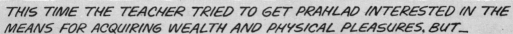

THIS TIME THE TEACHER TRIED TO GET PRAHLAD INTERESTED IN THE MEANS FOR ACQUIRING WEALTH AND PHYSICAL PLEASURES, BUT_

HOW CAN THE PURSUIT OF PHYSICAL PLEASURES AND WEALTH BRING HAPPINESS? IT WILL ONLY LEAD TO ENVY AND ANGER.

WHILE PRAHLAD WAS ENGAGED IN SUCH THOUGHTS, OTHER PUPILS CAME AND JOINED HIM.

PRAHLAD, TALK TO US ABOUT YOUR BELIEFS.

WORSHIP VISHNU. HE IS THE SOUL OF ALL CREATED BEINGS AND EXISTS EVERYWHERE.

O ASURAS, DIRECT YOUR DEVOTION TO VISHNU AND LOVE ALL CREATED BEINGS.

TELL US, PRAHLAD, WHERE DID YOU LEARN ALL THIS?

FROM THE SAGE NARADA.

AND PRAHLAD TOLD THEM THE STORY OF HIS BIRTH.

THE ASURA LADS LISTENED TO PRAHLAD AND ACCEPTED ALL HIS TEACHINGS.

WHAT OUR GURU HAS TAUGHT US IS NOT TRUE.

VISHNU IS THE SOUL...

AT THAT MOMENT THE TEACHER CAME OUT.

WHAT? WHAT ARE YOU SAYING?

THAT VISHNU IS THE SOUL OF ALL CREATED BEINGS AND IS PRESENT EVERYWHERE.

THE TEACHER WENT STRAIGHT TO HIRANYAKASHIPU.

O LORD, WE MUST DO SOMETHING BEFORE ANY MORE HARM IS DONE.

YOUR SON IS SPREADING HIS VILE BELIEFS AMONG MY PUPILS!

HIRANYAKASHIPU SENT FOR PRAHLAD.

YOU WICKED WRETCH! ARE YOU TRYING TO DESTROY ME AND MY RACE?

THE RULERS OF THE THREE WORLDS QUAKE BEFORE ME. BUT SPEAK UP, WHAT IS THE SOURCE OF YOUR POWER?

O FATHER! IT IS LORD VISHNU. HE IS THE SOURCE NOT ONLY OF MY POWER, BUT OF YOURS TOO AND OF ALL OTHER POWERFUL BEINGS!

IT IS OBVIOUS THAT YOU WISH TO DIE.

WHERE IS HE? IF HE IS EVERYWHERE WHY IS HE NOT IN THIS PILLAR?

IF HE IS NOT THERE I SHALL SEVER YOUR HEAD FROM YOUR TRUNK. LET VISHNU YOUR LORD, PROTECT...

AND LO! LORD VISHNU IN THE FORM OF *NARA-SIMHA EMERGED FROM THE PILLAR.

THIS IS NEITHER BEAST NOR MAN! WHAT IS THIS? IT ADVANCES TOWARDS ME...

NARA-SIMHA CAUGHT HIRANYA-KASHIPU AND...

IT IS THE TWILIGHT HOUR. I AM DOOMED.

...CARRIED HIM TO THE THRESHOLD OF THE COURTROOM.

ALAS WE ARE NEITHER INDOORS NOR OUTDOORS.

* HALF-MAN. HALF-LION.

THERE HE KILLED HIM.

THEN NARA-SIMHA SEATED HIMSELF ON HIRANYAKASHIPU'S THRONE.

BRAHMA AND INDRA CAME TO PAY HOMAGE TO HIM.

BUT WERE WARY OF APPROACHING VISHNU IN THIS TERRIFYING ASPECT.

THEN BRAHMA WENT TO PRAHLAD WHO WAS STANDING NEARBY.

O SON APPROACH AND PROPITIATE THE LORD!

SO BE IT.

NARA-SIMHA WAS TOUCHED.

O GREAT PRAHLAD! I AM PLEASED WITH YOU! ASK ME ANY BOON OF YOUR CHOICE.

I HAVE ALL I DESIRE. YOU HAVE ALLOWED ME TO TAKE REFUGE IN YOU.

BUT NARA-SIMHA INSISTED.

YET I WISH TO GRANT YOU A BOON.

THEN LET MY FATHER BE PURIFIED OF ALL HIS SINS.

BEING YOUR FATHER, HE IS ALREADY PURIFIED. REIGN IN HIS PLACE AND DO YOUR DUTIES.

SO BE IT.

NARA-SIMHA VANISHED. AND PRAHLAD BOWED TO BRAHMA AND TO THE OTHER CELESTIALS.

GO NOW AND PER-FORM THE LAST RITES OF YOUR FATHER, MY SON.

AFTER THE LAST RITES OF HIS FATHER WERE OVER, THE GODS WITH THE HELP OF THE ASURAS INSTALLED PRAHLAD ON THE THRONE AS LORD OF THE ASURAS. AND HE RULED WISELY AND WELL FOR MANY YEARS.

# Dhruva and Ashtavakra

Illustrated Classics From India

# Dhruva and Ashtavakra

The story of Dhruva is taken from the Bhagawat Purana. Dhruva was barely five years old when he performed penance to win the favour of Lord Narayana (Vishnu). Pleased with the faith of the child, Vishnu appeared before him and told him that he would rule the earth for 36,000 years and then occupy a very important place in heaven. And sure enough, to this day, Dhruva resides in the sky as the Pole star, referred to by many Hindus as the "Dhruva Tara" or "Dhruva Nakshatra".

According to the Vishnu Purana, the "Dhruva Nakshatra" occupies a significant position in the cosmos. It is placed at the tail of the porpoise-like celestial sphere with Lord Narayana at the centre, and, as it revolves, it causes the sun, the moon and the stars to revolve too.

The story of Ashtavakra is taken from the Mahabharata. While in exile, the Pandava princes, accompanied by Sage Lomasha, visited a number of holy places. When they reached the hermitage of Shwetaketu the sage told them the story of Ashtavakra, the nephew of Shwetaketu, who was born with eight physical deformities and overcame all odds with the gift of knowledge and sheer perseverance.

## Editor: Anant Pai
Script: Shailaja Ganguly and Malati Shenoy     Illustrations: Ram Waeerkar
Cover: Ramesh Umrotkar

# DHRUVA

DHRUVA WAS THE SON OF SUNEETI, THE SENIOR QUEEN OF KING UTTANAPADA. UNFORTUNATELY FOR DHRUVA AND SUNEETI, UTTANAPADA LOVED SURUCHI, HIS SECOND QUEEN, BETTER AND WAS PARTIAL TO HER.

AH! HERE COMES QUEEN SURUCHI.

HER ONE AIM IS TO SEE HER SON, UTTAMA, CROWNED KING. POOR DHRUVA.

AS SURUCHI WALKED UP TO HER SON—

MOTHER, FATHER IS FREE. MAY I GO AND SIT ON HIS LAP?

CERTAINLY, MY SON. IT IS YOUR RIGHTFUL PLACE AS THE FUTURE KING.

WHEN DHRUVA SAW UTTAMA SITTING ON UTTANAPADA'S LAP, HE RAN TOWARDS THEM.

CERTAINLY NOT!

I TOO WILL SIT ON MY FATHER'S LAP.

YOU HAVE NO RIGHT TO BE THERE. GO AWAY.

WHERE SHALL I GO, MOTHER?

GO TO LORD NARAYANA* AND SEEK HIS FAVOUR TO BE REBORN AS MY SON. ONLY THEN CAN YOU ENJOY THE SAME RIGHTS AS UTTAMA.

* ANOTHER NAME FOR VISHNU.

2

STUNG BY HER WORDS, DHRUVA RAN CRYING TO HIS MOTHER.

WHY ARE YOU CRYING, DHRUVA? HAS ANYONE HURT YOU?

MOTHER SURUCHI SAID I HAD NO RIGHT TO SIT ON MY FATHER'S LAP.

SHE SAID ONLY UTTAMA HAD THE RIGHT TO SIT ON THE KING'S LAP.

SHE'S RIGHT, DHRUVA.

HOLDING BACK HER TEARS, SUNEETI HUGGED HIM AND CARRIED HIM IN.

I AM A KSHATRIYA PRINCE, AM I NOT, MOTHER?

YES, MY CHILD.

SECURE IN HIS MOTHER'S ARMS, DHRUVA BECAME CALM AND THOUGHTFUL.

MOTHER, SURUCHI TOLD ME TO GO AND SEEK LORD NARAYANA'S FAVOUR IF I WANT TO SIT ON MY FATHER'S LAP.

WILL NARAYANA REALLY HELP ME, MOTHER?

YES, MY CHILD. HE NEVER FAILS THOSE WHO TURN TO HIM.

THEN I SHALL SEEK HIM OUT.

GO, MY SON. HE IS THE ONLY ONE WHO CAN HELP US. IT WILL NOT BE EASY TO FIND HIM. BUT IF YOU TRY HARD ENOUGH YOU WILL SUCCEED.

I WILL SUCCEED, MOTHER. I WILL NOT RETURN TILL I MEET THE LORD. I WILL BECOME A GREATER KING THAN MY FATHER OR HIS FATHER BEFORE HIM.

MEANWHILE, SAGE NARADA CAME TO KNOW ABOUT SURUCHI'S HARSH WORDS AND DHRUVA'S RESOLVE.

HE IS A TRUE KSHATRIYA INDEED. THOUGH A MERE CHILD, HE WILL NOT BROOK THE INSULTS OF HIS STEP-MOTHER. YET WHAT HE SEEKS IS IMPOSSIBLE. I MUST SPEAK TO HIM.

NARADA WENT TO SEE DHRUVA.

MY CHILD, WHY DON'T YOU ACCEPT YOUR FATE AND GO BACK TO YOUR MOTHER?

O MASTER, I AM DHRUVA, THE SON OF MIGHTY UTTANAPADA, A KSHATRIYA. AND I AM DETERMINED TO WIN THE LORD'S FAVOUR.

I AM AWARE OF THAT, MY CHILD. BUT YOU ARE TOO YOUNG. IT IS NOT EASY TO FIND LORD NARAYANA. WHY DON'T YOU WAIT TILL YOU ARE A LITTLE OLDER?

FORGIVE ME, MASTER, BUT I WILL NOT TURN BACK. O WISE ONE, TELL ME HOW I CAN SUCCEED IN MY RESOLVE.

NARADA WAS EXTREMELY PLEASED BY HIS DETERMINATION.

IF YOU MEDITATE IN THE MADHUVAN FOREST ON THE BANKS OF THE YAMUNA, YOU WILL FIND THE LORD.

O SAINT, TEACH ME HOW TO MEDITATE.

REPEAT WITH ME — *OM NAMO BHAGAWATE VASUDEVAYA!

OM NAMO BHAGAWATE VASUDEVAYA.

SAY THAT OVER AND OVER AGAIN, AND CONCENTRATE ON THAT.

AS DHRUVA SET OUT FOR MADHUVAN, NARADA WENT TO THE PALACE OF KING UTTANAPADA.

WELCOME! WELCOME, SAGE NARADA. PLEASE BE SEATED.

NARADA NOTICED THAT THOUGH UTTANA-PADA WELCOMED HIM RESPECTFULLY, HIS MIND WAS ELSEWHERE.

O KING, WHAT ARE YOU THINKING ABOUT?

HOLY SAGE, I AM THE VILEST OF MEN. I DID NOT UTTER A WORD WHEN SURUCHI DROVE POOR DHRUVA AWAY WITH HER CRUEL WORDS.

ALAS! HE HAS GONE AWAY ALONE INTO THE FOREST. THE BEASTS WILL DEVOUR HIM.

FEAR NOT, O KING. THE LORD HIM-SELF WILL PROTECT YOUR SON. HE WILL COME BACK BRINGING GLORY TO ALL.

* I BOW TO THE REVERED VASUDEVA (VISHNU).

6

MEANWHILE, DHRUVA HAD REACHED MADHUVAN.

I SHALL SIT HERE AND BEGIN MY MEDITATION.

IN THE FIRST MONTH, HE LIVED ONLY ON THE FRUITS HE COULD FIND IN THE FOREST.

GRADUALLY HE GAVE UP EVEN THAT AND ATE ONLY GRASS AND LEAVES.

IN THE THIRD MONTH, HE STOPPED EATING AND LIVED ONLY ON WATER.

IN THE FOURTH MONTH, HE GAVE UP EVEN THAT AND LIVED ON AIR. THROUGHOUT THE PERIOD HE REPEATED THE MANTRA OVER AND OVER AGAIN.

OM NAMO BHAGAVATE VASUDEVAYA!

IN THE FIFTH AND SIXTH MONTHS, HE EVEN STOPPED BREATHING.

OM NAMO BHAGAVATE VASUDEVAYA.

DHRUVA'S CONCENTRATION STOPPED THE VERY AIR FROM FLOWING. THERE WAS PANIC IN HEAVEN...

MEANWHILE, AS DHRUVA MEDITATED —

LORD, I THOUGHT I HAD FOUND YOU BUT YOU'VE SUDDENLY VANISHED. HAVE I FAILED IN MY WORSHIP? HAVE I DISPLEASED YOU? THEN I SHALL START MEDITATING ALL OVER AGAIN.

AND DHRUVA OPENED HIS EYES.

THE LORD HAS COME TO ME!

*THE POLE STAR TO THIS DAY IS KNOWN AS DHRUVA.

QUEEN SUNEETI STEPPED FORWARD.

O MY SON, MY GLORIOUS SON!

AND AMIDST GREAT REJOICING, DHRUVA WAS CARRIED BACK TO THE PALACE. AS SOON AS DHRUVA WAS OLD ENOUGH TO RULE, UTTANAPADA CROWNED HIM KING AND RETIRED TO THE FOREST.

# ASHTAVAKRA

KAHODA WAS THE FAVOURITE DISCIPLE OF UDDALAKA, A RENOWNED SCHOLAR IN THE VEDAS. UDDALAKA HAD A DAUGHTER CALLED SUJATA.

ONE DAY— I AM PLEASED WITH YOUR DEVOTION, KAHODA. AS SOON AS YOU HAVE MASTERED THE SACRED TEXTS...

...YOU SHALL HAVE MY DAUGHTER, SUJATA, FOR A WIFE

KAHODA WAS CLEVER AND HARD-WORKING AND SOON MASTERED THE TEXTS. AS HIS GURU HAD PROMISED HE WAS MARRIED TO SUJATA.

YOU MAY CONTINUE TO LIVE HERE AT THE ASHRAM, AND TEACH YOUR DISCIPLES.

THOUGH THEY HAD TO LEAD AN AUSTERE LIFE, KAHODA AND SUJATA WERE HAPPY IN SAGE UDDALAKA'S HERMITAGE.

MY LORD, WHEN WE HAVE A SON, HE MUST MASTER THE SACRED TEXTS AS YOU HAVE.

I SHALL SPARE NO PAINS TO TEACH HIM ALL I KNOW.

A FEW MONTHS LATER, SUJATA BECAME PREGNANT.

I MUST EXPOSE MY CHILD TO THE SACRED INFLUENCE OF THE HYMNS EVEN WHILE HE IS IN THE WOMB.

SO SUJATA SAT BY HER HUSBAND AS HE RECITED VERSES FROM THE SCRIPTURES; AND THE CHILD IN HER WOMB SILENTLY ABSORBED WHAT THE LEARNED FATHER RECITED.

ONE DAY AS KAHODA SAT AMONG HIS DISCIPLES, INSTRUCTING THEM—

THAT'S NOT THE WAY TO CHANT THAT HYMN, FATHER.

WHO WAS THAT? WHERE DID THAT VOICE COME FROM?

IT MUST HAVE BEEN THE VOICE OF OUR UNBORN CHILD.

SUCH IMPERTINENCE! AND FROM ONE YET UNBORN!

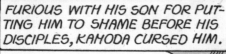

FURIOUS WITH HIS SON FOR PUTTING HIM TO SHAME BEFORE HIS DISCIPLES, KAHODA CURSED HIM.

O VAIN SOUL! MAY YOU BE BORN DEFORMED— MAY YOUR BODY BE TWISTED IN EIGHT PLACES!

THE MONTHS ROLLED ON AND THE TIME FOR SUJATA'S CONFINEMENT DREW NEAR. ONE DAY—

OUR CHILD WILL SOON BE BORN. WE WILL NEED MONEY TO PROVIDE IT WITH THE COMFORTS OF LIFE.

I WILL GO TO KING JANAKA OF MITHILA. HE IS GENEROUS TO LEARNED BRAHMANS. BESIDES, HE IS AT THE MOMENT PERFORMING A GRAND YAGNA.

WHEN KAHODA REACHED MITHILA, JANAKA WELCOMED HIM.

O REVERED SAGE, YOU HAVE COME AT THE RIGHT MOMENT.

A SCHOLAR NAMED BANDHI HAS COME TO MITHILA. NO ONE CAN DEFEAT HIM IN DEBATE.

LET ME TRY, O KING.

THINK IT OVER CAREFULLY. THOUGH YOU WILL BE WELL REWARDED IF YOU WIN...

...YOU WILL BE DROWNED IN THE RIVER IF YOU DON'T. AND MANY SCHOLARS HAVE LOST THEIR LIVES.

I ACCEPT THE CHALLENGE.

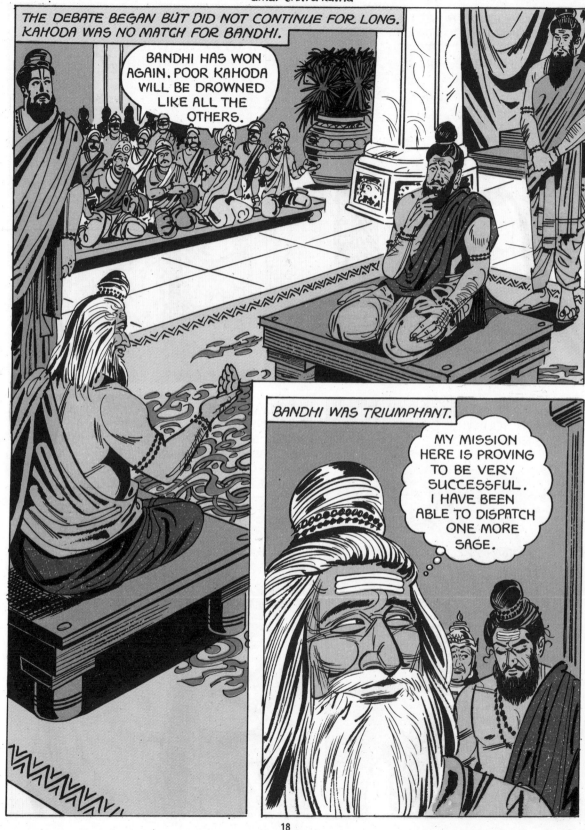

THE DEBATE BEGAN BUT DID NOT CONTINUE FOR LONG. KAHODA WAS NO MATCH FOR BANDHI.

BANDHI HAS WON AGAIN. POOR KAHODA WILL BE DROWNED LIKE ALL THE OTHERS.

BANDHI WAS TRIUMPHANT.

MY MISSION HERE IS PROVING TO BE VERY SUCCESSFUL. I HAVE BEEN ABLE TO DISPATCH ONE MORE SAGE.

BUT JANAKA WAS UNHAPPY.

ALAS! I HAVE LOST ONE MORE SAGE WHO CAME TO ATTEND THE YAGNA. HOW WILL THE YAGNA BE A SUCCESS?

WHEN THE NEWS REACHED SUJATA, SHE BROKE DOWN.

ALAS! MY DESIRE FOR WEALTH HAS COST ME MY HUSBAND AND MY CHILD ITS FATHER.

DON'T GRIEVE, SUJATA. YOUR CHILD SHALL NOT LACK A FATHER'S LOVE.

A FEW DAYS LATER SUJATA HAD A BABY.

ALAS! HIS BODY IS DEFORMED IN EIGHT PLACES.

LET HIM BE CALLED ASHTAVAKRA*. MY WIFE TOO HAS JUST BEEN BLESSED WITH A SON. WE HAVE NAMED HIM SHWETAKETU.

GROWING UP UNDER THE TENDER, LOVING CARE OF UDDALAKA...

* CROOKED IN EIGHT PLACES.

...ASHTAVAKRA SOON BEGAN TO LOOK UPON HIM AS HIS FATHER.

THE YEARS ROLLED ON. UDDALAKA TAUGHT ASHTA-VAKRA AND SHWETAKETU.

WHEN THE BOYS WERE TWELVE YEARS OLD—

YOU HAVE MASTERED THE VEDAS. I AM PROUD OF YOU, MY SON.

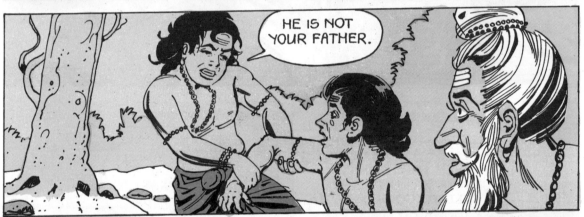

AND SUJATA TOLD HIM ALL THAT HAD HAPPENED.

I MUST DEFEAT BANDHI AND HAVE HIM DROWNED.

THAT NIGHT—

COME ON, SHWETAKETU. LET US GO TO MITHILA. IT WILL BE A GOOD EXPERIENCE FOR US. KING JANAKA HAS NOT BEEN ABLE TO COMPLETE THE YAGNA HE STARTED TWELVE YEARS AGO.

SHWETAKETU WAS WILLING.

WHEN DO YOU WANT TO LEAVE?

AT ONCE.

22

WHEN THE BOYS REACHED THE GATES OF JANAKA'S PALACE AT MITHILA—

WHO ARE YOU? WHAT DO YOU WANT?

WE HAVE COME TO MEET THE KING. PLEASE TAKE US TO HIM.

THE KING IS PERFORMING A YAGNA. I HAVE BEEN ORDERED TO PERMIT ONLY OLD LEARNED BRAHMANS TO SEE HIM.

TO POSSESS TRUE KNOWLEDGE ONE NEED NOT BE GREY-HAIRED OR BALD. IT IS WRONG TO JUDGE A MAN'S MERIT BY HIS AGE. I MAY BE YOUNG BUT I HAVE OBSERVED THE SACRED VOWS AND HAVE MASTERED THE VEDAS.

THE BOYS WERE TAKEN TO JANAKA.

O KING, I HAVE HEARD OF BANDHI'S CHALLENGE AND THE FATE OF THOSE WHO FAILED TO MEET IT. I HAVE COME TO CHALLENGE BANDHI AND TO SEE HIM DESTROYED.

JANAKA WAS ASTONISHED.

HE IS JUST A CHILD. IT IS MY DUTY TO WARN HIM.

YOU SPEAK OF DEFEATING BANDHI BECAUSE YOU ARE IGNORANT OF HIS SKILL IN DEBATE. NO ONE HAS BEEN ABLE TO DEFEAT HIM.

THAT'S BECAUSE HE WAS NEVER CONFRONTED WITH A SCHOLAR OF MY CALIBRE. I WILL NOT GO BACK TILL I SEE HIM DEFEATED AND DROWNED.

WHEN JANAKA SAW THAT ASHTAVAKRA WAS ADAMANT—

THE BOY IS CONFIDENT. I WILL TEST HIS INTELLIGENCE BY ASKING HIM A FEW QUESTIONS.

IF YOU CAN ANSWER MY QUESTIONS I WILL LET YOU MEET BANDHI.

WHAT IS IT THAT DOES NOT MOVE WHEN BORN?

AN EGG.

BANDHI HAS MET HIS MATCH. LET ASHTAVAKRA DECIDE HIS FATE.

BANDHI HAD THOSE WHOM HE DEFEATED THROWN INTO THE RIVER. LET HIM MEET WITH THE SAME FATE TODAY.

DROWN HIM!

SEIZE HIM!

BANDHI STEPPED FORWARD.

O KING! I AM THE SON OF VARUNA.* THE SAGES I DEFEATED ARE NOT DEAD. MY FATHER WAS PERFORMING A YAGNA FOR WHICH HE NEEDED SAGES FROM THE EARTH. THE CHALLENGE WAS A MEANS OF SENDING THEM TO HIM.

THE YAGNA MUST BE OVER BY NOW AND THEY SHOULD RETURN. AND BY ASHTAVAKRA'S GRACE I CAN GO BACK TO MY FATHER. LET US GO TO THE RIVER.

*LORD OF THE HYDROSPHERE.

NOW WITH YOUR PERMISSION, O KING, I WILL GO BACK TO MY FATHER'S KINGDOM.

THEN AS THEY WATCHED, BANDHI JUMPED INTO THE WATER...

KAHODA, ASHTAVAKRA AND SHWETAKETU RETURNED TO THE HERMITAGE. AS SOON AS THEY ARRIVED THERE, KAHODA TOOK SUJATA AND ASHTAVAKRA TO THE RIVER FLOWING NEAR BY.

ASHTAVAKRA, TAKE A QUICK PLUNGE INTO THE RIVER AND COME OUT.

ASHTAVAKRA DID AS HE WAS TOLD. A SECOND LATER, AS HE EMERGED FROM THE WATER—

MOTHER! FATHER! LOOK! MY BODY! IT'S NO LONGER DEFORMED!

THEY WENT TO UDDALAKA.

LOOK FATHER! ASHTAVAKRA'S BODY IS NO LONGER DEFORMED!

UDDALAKA REJOICED TO SEE HIS GRANDSON'S BODY STRAIGHT AND TALL. THE HERMITAGE ONCE AGAIN BECAME THE HAVEN OF PEACE IT USED TO BE.

Illustrated Classics from India

# NOW AVAILABLE ONLINE!

The magic of the colourful tales of Amar Chitra Katha has woven nostalgic bonds amo
the Indian diaspora all over the globe. The Amar Chitra Katha comic books help India
remain tethered to their roots, while making their mark as citizens of the world.

Order from the complete catalogue at a special online price, and also access heaps o
information on Indian heritage and culture.

## www.AmarChitraKatha.com

INDIA BOOK HOUSE

Mahalaxmi Chambers, 5th Floor, 22 Bhulabhai Desai Road, Mumbai 400 026, India
Tel 23523827  Fax 23538406  Email info@amarchitrakatha.com